I Am Priceless:
Voices of Victory Over Violence

Compiled by Regina Rowley

Co-authored by:

Alison Pourteau, M.A.
Licensed Professional Counselor-Supervisor

Cathy Fields

Debra Coody, D.C.

Raquel Masco

Kimberlee A. Parmer, MS, LCDC
Licensed Professional Counselor Intern

Danyelle Potter

Carolee Madron Ayres

Diana Solis

I Am Priceless: Voices of Victory Over Violence

I Am Priceless: Voices of Victory Over Violence

1.Self Help 2. Abuse

ISBN-10: 153705189X
ISBN-13: 978-1537051895
Self-Help / Abuse / General

TABLE OF CONTENTS

Note from Regina:

The root of the word courage, cor means heart. Courage: implies firmness of mind and will in the face of danger or extreme difficulty. It takes great courage to bare your soul and be a Voice of Victory over Violence. It takes immense courage to face the fear and shame of skeletons still lurking in the closet; to remove the shabby bandages of yesteryear covering festering wounds; to dig deep, clean out and air the wounds in order for them to heal. It takes dedicated firmness of mind and will to face fears and break free! To build beautiful stepping stones from the skeletons... we share our hearts and declare, No More Silence!

Maya Angelou so aptly states: "There is no greater agony than bearing an untold story inside you."

These stories are raw, unpolished accounts of strong, victorious women. They are shared from the depth of our hearts. We are women who feel, struggle and doubt, just like you. We are women who recognize We Are Priceless and have chosen to #HealForward.

Each author has courageously revisited her experiences in order to be a Voice of Victory. This process has been painful and difficult. Effects from the process, for some, have led to chronic pain or relapses in our health. It is our hope, you will read our stories with compassion and understanding, recognizing the struggles involved in conveying our deepest hurts, so you will know, you really aren't alone on this #HealingForward journey.

While none of us can go back to change our circumstances, like Terri St. Cloud expresses, "She could never go back and make some of the details pretty. All she could do was move forward and make the whole beautiful." www.bonesigharts.com; we have chosen to make our 'whole beautiful'. We invite you to join us. For a supportive community as you move forward, meet us at www.IAm-Priceless.org

Dear Reader, Above all remember, You Are Priceless!

Disclaimer: Each author had the liberty to change identifying details, including names, relationships, while maintaining the integrity of her story. Any resemblance to actual persons, events, and entities is entirely coincidental.

Forward for I Am Priceless, Voices of Victory Over Violence

To find and use one's voice in the midst of pain, darkness and despair is a distinctive measure of courage and leadership. So often individuals, women in particular, are held captive as prisoners in their own beliefs. Cycles of abuse, violence and harassment are accepted and tolerated, without resistance, without question. A shift in power occurs, making them (and maybe you) a victim by carrying a belief that you are not worthy or deserving of more. *I Am Priceless, Voices of Victory Over Violence* is the light at the end of that tunnel. It is your resource to see what is truly possible in reclaiming your personal power.

As a child of domestic abuse, myself, I found I created behaviors and cycles as a way to cope. I had convinced myself that I deserved the verbal and emotional abuse, somehow. You see, I carried a belief that I deserved to get knocked down, to be a human "punching bag," and that what didn't kill me truly made me stronger. As a result, I sought out environments throughout a good portion of my life after that, personally and professionally, that continued that cycle.

I took hit after hit, word after word, always finding a way to bounce back … though, sometimes not so quickly. I felt I had to fight for everything, to prove something. It was that tough love approach I told myself, and truly believed, was the only way for me to survive. I held a strong conviction back then that I was stronger for not talking about my childhood, not talking about my relationship with my dad, or about the impact he had on our family. I thought it made me a victim to talk about it. And, I was adamant that I ***was not*** going to be a victim.

Sound familiar? We create these "truths," these misconceptions, about what really is. So, for me, I kept all of it bottled up and to myself. I toughened up. I wanted to shut everyone out, fight anyone who wanted to dig deeper, and didn't let anyone really get close. I refused to be vulnerable and let anyone see what really was going on. Again, I was convinced I wasn't a victim. I firmly thought I was strong, better than what was going on around me.

Little did I know that keeping these things quiet created a different kind of victim mentality. These secrets were my anchor, my skeletons. What I finally realized was all of this actually made me the victim I was so determined not to be; that all of this created a survivor type mentality. I also realize I was exhausted with the fight. When I gave myself permission to be fully honest with myself, to be vulnerable, I finally had an awakening and realized I wanted more for myself and for my life.

I realize that I now wanted to thrive, to free myself from the shackles and skeletons in my own closet. As did the women whose stories you will read about here in this incredibly beautiful compilation that Regina Rowley so passionately and purposefully brought together.

For in this anthology, you will meet some of the most amazing women who have stepped fully into their fear, have found their voice, and have courageously chosen to share their stories. These women, these survivors, these thrivers, will inspire you to find your own voice, to find your own personal power as they demonstrate how they dug deep within themselves to find the light and allow themselves to finally break free.

This is YOUR time to shine! This is your guide, your tool, to open the doors to the closet you have been locked behind! This is your time to liberate yourself and find your freedom! We all have choices. Being a survivor is a choice. Being a victim is a choice. But, so is being a thriver and being a voice! Because how you choose to show up, how you choose to serve others, and how you choose to take personal responsibility inside those two spaces is all a choice you *get* to make.

Once you choose to release yourself from those emotional attachments, offer forgiveness and stay in a place of pure gratitude, you release yourself from the demons, from the skeletons, and truly find your peace to create your own happiness. *I Am Priceless, Voices of Victory Over Violence* is YOUR launching pad to free yourself once and for all, to find your voice and to reclaim your power fully.

It's time for you to say YES to yourself, to stand up and stand out fully with the gifts and love God gave you.

May you find peace, grace, power and love in your journey!

With great love and healing energy,

- Candy

Candy Barone
CEO & Founder of You Empowered Strong, LLC
Author of *You Empowered Strong; Infinite Possibilities in the Power of YES* and *Dream Star*

You are a hero, because you are changing the world by saying no to abuse.

Domestic Violence Survivor

Alison Pourteau, M.A.
Licensed Professional
Counselor-Supervisor

Scars of the Heart:
Surviving the Invisible Wounds of Emotional Abuse

Abuse isn't a single act. It's not an isolated argument, or even recurring arguments, ending in tears and blood and bruises. It's a way of interacting, day after day, across a spectrum of life experiences that keeps the most significant person in the abuser's life under their control. The victim is made to feel not only powerless and vulnerable, but also to feel guilty, ashamed, confused, and made to believe they're going crazy. They live in fear and feel depressed and look to themselves for a reason for, and a solution to, the abuse. To better understand what life at the hands of an abuser would be like, let's look at Rebecca's story.

Rebecca met Shawn over 15 years ago. They were married for 10 years and had one child together. It was not until their separation and eventual divorce that Rebecca began to accept that Shawn had abused her. "Even after he was gone, I swore to people, including his family, that he had never abused me," she says. "I even believed it. As if hitting me was the worst thing he could do."

What Abuse Is Really All About

There are many types of abuse, just as there are many types of victims and abusers. The basis of any abusive relationship is power and control. Establishing *power over* in a relationship can certainly be achieved effectively through physical power. When most people think of abuse, the first thing that pops into their heads is someone— usually a woman—being punched, slapped, kicked, or suffering some other form of physical violence, typically at the hands of a male partner. Based on my experience working with victims of domestic violence, the most common types of abuse are also the least understood by the public and helping professionals alike. These forms of abuse don't leave bruises or visible marks. They can be committed in front of others and no one but the victim realizes it's happening; or, if observers do realize something is amiss, they're usually too polite to say anything or simply don't want to get involved. Worst of all, the victim often doesn't even realize that they're being abused.

Abusers can be incredibly adept at figuring out just what to do or say to impact or influence the person they're with. Very often, this process starts early in the relationship. Rebecca describes her first memory of one of Shawn's angry outbursts. (Note: although this example is of a heterosexual couple, with a male abuser, it should be understood that the same interactions and abuses occur regardless of gender or sexual orientation.)

"Shawn seemed like the ideal partner," Rebecca remembers, "the kind of person I'd always dreamed of. Not only was he intelligent and nice looking, he was attentive and charming and wanted to know everything about me, good and bad." The relationship progressed quickly, largely because Shawn told Rebecca, over and over again, how perfect they were together. "He called us soul mates and said he wanted to spend every free moment with me. I was flattered to have someone be so devoted." Six months after they met, Rebecca moved into Shawn's apartment with him. "It was his idea," she says, "but I was ready to live without roommates, to be a *real* adult. He said it made sense for us to live at his place rather than have to pay a deposit on a new one and that I would add a much-needed feminine touch."

The Red Flags

Rebecca was excited on her first day in *their* apartment together. She spent the day unpacking her belongings and trying to merge their possessions. Rebecca states, "I wanted to add that feminine touch Shawn kept talking about and make the apartment ours. He always insisted on calling it *ours* as soon as I agreed to move in. It was very much a bachelor pad, but I tried really hard to make our stuff work together, to make it a place for both of us."

Looking around the apartment at the end of a long day, she was very pleased with what she had accomplished. She felt like the apartment was not exactly what she would choose for herself, but it was a nice compromise for the present. She had just finished working and had collapsed onto the couch when Shawn came home from work.

"I went from super excited to extremely anxious in a matter of seconds. A look of hatred came over his face and he just stood there and glared at me. Then he began yelling, '*What have you done?*' I just stood there stunned. Shawn started accusing me of throwing out his stuff to make room for mine. I tried to explain that I hadn't thrown anything out, I'd just moved things around—but he wouldn't listen. He just kept yelling over my explanations, accusing me of not caring about his input and taking over *his* apartment. He called me self-centered and selfish. Those words hurt me so deeply. He had always told me before how much he loved my generosity and willingness to give to others."

It Must Have Been Something I Did

When Rebecca tried to defend herself, Shawn simply ignored her and continued yelling at her about how he'd worked all day while she was sitting at home and that she couldn't even be bothered to make dinner for them. "He finally just stormed out of the apartment. I just stood there, shocked and devastated. I spent the next few hours, playing the scene over and over in my mind, trying to figure out what I'd done wrong: *I shouldn't have moved his stuff around. Maybe I should have waited until he was home to unpack. I should have thought about him working all day and how nice it would be for him to come home to a home-cooked meal.* I moved all his things back to where they'd been and put mine back in boxes. I kept wondering what I was going to do if he didn't want me to move in with him after all. My roommates had already made plans with another friend to take over my portion of my old apartment. I felt as if my world had turned upside down in a matter of moments."

Rebecca eventually cried herself to sleep and only woke up when she heard Shawn crawl into bed next to her. She was too nervous to try talking to him, so she just lay there, trying to go back to sleep. "The next day, Shawn apologized for 'making a big deal out of something minor.' He said that he was just stressed out about work and feeling vulnerable about taking the next step in our relationship. I apologized for not getting his input before making decisions about how to decorate the apartment and promised that I would make dinner from now on any time I was off. Shawn just kind of brushed that aside, saying it wasn't necessary, but I made sure to get groceries and have dinner ready that night. I didn't want to take a chance of having another evening together end as badly as the first."

The second night in their new apartment together went much better than the first, just as Rebecca had hoped. Any concerns or red flags that something might not be right with this relationship were quickly swept aside. However, what had happened continued to plague Rebecca. She always made sure to consult with Shawn before rearranging the furniture or changing up the décor in any way. She was also very dutiful in her efforts to make dinner for the two of them, especially on her days off. As tightly as Rebecca tried to lock away the memories of Shawn's blow-up and how hurt she felt, the effects remained with her.

As most victims do, she looked to herself to fix the problem. She accepted Shawn's excuses for his behavior, and began making excuses for him herself. "I felt that if I could just explain myself more clearly, if I could just get Shawn to understand my intentions, he wouldn't feel this way, he wouldn't get so mad." But he did keep getting mad, and every time he did, she would accept his apology, shove the memory away to a far corner of her mind, and focus on keeping him in a good mood that day, trying even harder to get everything right. She thought that—if she were patient enough, devoted enough, tried hard enough—they would have the life they had dreamed of together. She could have the "nice Shawn" around all the time. Despite her best efforts over the years to change herself and her behaviors in order to make Shawn happy, there were many more blowups and more hurt feelings than she could ever recount.

Not All Bruises Are on the Outside

Looking back over the marriage, Rebecca explains, "I can tell you the words he used a lot at the end: whore and slut and bitch. But it was never that blatant through most of the marriage. He never came straight out and called me stupid or lazy, but I can tell you how he made me feel. I wasn't enough. I wasn't successful enough, moral enough, hardworking enough. I didn't put my family first the way I should. I was self-centered and egotistical. I was always saying and doing the wrong things. I couldn't be trusted to remember anything, whether it was to lock up the house or clean the kitchen correctly. It's sad that I can't remember exactly what he said, but even now, I still hear his yelling, critical voice in my head."

One of the most insidious forms of abuse men like Shawn, or any abuser, will perpetrate is verbal in nature. When most of us think of verbal abuse, we think of someone being called horrible names; and while this certainly happens, often abuse is more subtle—more difficult to recognize and more difficult to explain. So often, the injury is inflicted by a tone of voice, a sarcastic comment, or long periods of silence (aka, "the silent treatment"), even if the abuser insists nothing is wrong. In my work with victims of domestic violence, I've talked with many women who've experienced both verbal and physical abuse. Except for extreme, life-threatening situations, virtually every victim I talk to about their abuse feels the verbal component was the most painful experience. I hear such statements as "the bruises have healed. It's the words I can't get out of my head."

Rebecca's experience is typical. "I read his expressions, his silences, his footsteps. If he wasn't smiling and obviously in a good mood, I had to be on my guard. Had I done something wrong? What could I do to make him happy, to appease him? Even if everything seemed OK, you never knew when that might change—what simple, unexpected thing might set him off. I felt like I was stepping around in a mine field and constantly worried about setting the next landmine off."

Mood Management: A Strategy for Survival

Partners naturally tend to become experts about their significant others: what their favorite foods are, what they find irritating. In abusive relationships, the abuser uses their personal knowledge of the victim to hurt them. They know exactly where to stick the knife and just how far they can turn it without the victim fighting back. In turn, the victim becomes an expert in reading the moods and emotions of the abuser. Is he calm or irritated? What is his body language? What are his actions saying, and is it different from his words?

"I could walk into the kitchen and point out a hundred things he wanted done in a specific way," Rebecca says. "He said he wasn't even asking for anything major. Why couldn't I respect him enough to do the small things he asked? But there were so many *small things*, I just couldn't remember them all. I still get anxious and frustrated just thinking about it."

As with Shawn and Rebecca, abusive relationships usually don't start out that way, and they aren't without their good days in-between the bad. Blowups and arguments may be relatively few and far between; the verbal abuse, however, is much more consistent. It just tends to be subtle, like water wearing away a beautiful statue. Piece by piece, miniscule holes appear and tiny flecks chip away. It happens so gradually that you get used to the changes, until one day you look in the mirror and don't recognize the person you've become or what happened to the person you used to be. You doubt your own thoughts and perceptions. You might even doubt your own sanity.

"We were visiting with a neighbor once and the man made us cherry martinis," remembers Rebecca. "I thought they were delicious and when he asked me if I wanted another, I said yes. Later, when we got home, my husband told me that I'd licked my lips when I said yes and that it was extremely provocative. He was always telling me how he trusted me but he didn't trust other men. At the same time, he would tell me that some behavior or other was flirtatious or provocative. I wasn't trying to flirt with anyone. How do you fix your behavior when you don't recognize what you're doing wrong?"

As happens in many abusive relationships, Rebecca assumed that Shawn was seeing something she didn't. She took his word for it that "Every man will see it this way." As he had trained her to do over the years, she looked to herself as the source of the problem and tried to determine how she could fix it rather than realize the truth of the situation—that most men did not see the world, or her actions, the way Shawn would have her believe.

Jealousy is one of the most common characteristics of an abusive relationship. It allows the abuser not only an excuse to be angry but a reason to isolate the victim. For example, he may tell her, "Sure, you can go out with your sisters," but he texts and calls all night, checking up on her. Or he's surly and uncommunicative when she comes home (the silent treatment again). He may question where they went and whom she talked to, saying once again that he trusts her, but he doesn't trust any other man out there. The next time her sisters want to go out, she's likely to make an excuse not to go, just so she won't have to deal with the interrogation that follows.

Social settings aren't the only potential place for the abuser to obsess over. "He accused me of not opening up to him or telling him about what was going on at work; but when I did, there was always something going on he didn't approve of. He always seemed to be telling me what I needed to be doing differently and then, when I tried to do what he suggested, he told me what I did was wrong. It was all so ridiculous! I was so incredulous, I would just stand there with this stupid smile on my face, like I wanted to burst out laughing, though I felt like crying. It's like the wires in my brain that controlled my emotions and reactions were all tangled up. I was scared and exhausted and I wanted to scream, all at the same time. And he'd get even angrier because of that stupid smile on my face."

Falling Down the Rabbit Hole

One of the terms used a lot in discussing domestic violence—particularly verbal abuse—is "crazy-making" or "gaslighting." The term comes from the 1938 play, *Gas Light*—you might be more familiar with the Ingrid Berman movie version, 1944's *Gaslight*—in which a husband goes to great lengths to convince his wife that she's insane. I've had clients describe how their partner would deliberately switch movies around, putting them in the wrong cases, or move things in the kitchen and then accuse them of being disorganized and losing everything. For example, a wife might tell her husband she plans to visit her parents next week, making him angry; he proceeds to accuse her of obviously not wanting him along since she didn't even ask him to go and insists she cares more about her parents than her own children. The wife feels blindsided by his statement (since he's made it clear in the past he prefers not to visit her family) and she always takes the children with her. Later, when she tries to talk to him about his reaction, he tells her that she's overreacting and is always so sensitive, that her feelings get hurt over the slightest things. There are rarely direct answers from him to her questions about the incident. Conversations seem to run in circles, the history of what was said gets re-written; but always the fault for discord in the relationship is the victim's fault: she misunderstood, is too sensitive, or just plain wrong.

"I couldn't tell you what exactly he said to me that made me feel so miserable," says Rebecca. "He didn't start actually calling me names until the very end. But along the way, it was subtle things that were so hard to explain to other people. Simple things that, in and of themselves just didn't seem like a big deal. He would talk about a movie and if I said, 'Oh, I haven't seen that one,' he would tell me that I had and I just didn't remember. I *never* remembered, apparently. He always talked about how he couldn't find anything because of me and my piles, but he was a hoarder and brought so much stuff into the house, the only way I could attempt to keep it cleaned and organized was to pile his stuff up!"

Verbal abuse takes its toll, little by little, like the water eroding that beautiful statue. It steals away a person's self-worth and self-esteem. I have seen strong, independent, intelligent women whose self-confidence has been so completely destroyed, they have a difficult time making such simple decisions as what groceries to buy or what movie to watch. Attractive, athletic women are too embarrassed and self-conscious to exercise in public or wear sleeveless shirts. Patient, attentive mothers carry an intense feeling of guilt, believing they are not being a good enough parent to their children. All because their abuser convinced them it was so.

Always on the Radar

"Shawn would expect me to be home any time he was, preferably in the same room. I thought my 2-year-old could be clingy! I couldn't even get up to go to the bathroom without him asking where I was going! I was always so relieved when he had to work late. It gave me some time to myself, but I'd stay alert for his tires hitting the driveway. When I heard him pull up, I'd make sure to change the channel to something he'd consider appropriate or run to the kitchen and start cleaning. It felt like everything I did or said was subject to scrutiny. Even my emotions were analyzed, and usually found to be *wrong*.

"The only reprieve I could find were the few moments I had alone in the shower every morning. After all, who would notice the tears there? But after a while, even crying in the shower wasn't an option. Shawn would sneak into the tiny bathroom and be waiting there when I got out. I would open the curtain, and there he was. If he'd heard me crying, he'd ask what was wrong. He might have even sounded concerned or sympathetic. I wracked my brain for a safe answer, but what answer could I possibly give that would be safe? I decided on a vague one. 'I'm just not happy,' I said once, and his temper erupted: 'Well, it's all your fault!' and the latest lecture would began."

Over time, every aspect of a person's life can feel under their partner's inspection and control. Victims walk on eggshells, trying to avoid saying or doing anything that will start an argument. It may not even be out of fear, necessarily, of their partner. Their caution could stem from a desire to protect the children from witnessing a scene or because they're worn out from a long day at work and just don't have the energy to face a long, drawn-out disagreement. Many of my clients talk about the agony and frustration of being kept up, late into the night, by a partner who will not let an argument drop. In fact, sleep deprivation is a torture technique for extracting information from terrorists. These late nights seem to occur most frequently when the victim has to be up early the next day for work or with their children, leaving her even more physically and emotionally drained than before.

Money as a Means of Power and Control

Power and control can take many forms, such as financial abuse. I see this most often in situations where the husband is the primary breadwinner, but it's certainly not limited to these situations. Besides the unfair nature of one partner getting to spend money freely while the other must ask permission to spend money on the barest of necessities, this form of *command and control* adds another layer of stress and shame to the victim's life. For example, I had a client whose husband allowed her $50 a week for groceries and household supplies to provide for a family of four. Another client described how she had to turn to friends in order to buy basic feminine necessities, and then encountered an angry reaction from her husband when he found out. These were not families in poverty. There was plenty of money to cover each family's basic needs, but the abuser's desires came first. The victim will often sacrifice her own needs for the sake of the household, especially the children, and the abuser will continue spending money as he sees fit. In addition, being able to tell her what she can and cannot buy, or forcing her to ask him for money, keeps the balance of power one-sided.

"Shawn would never make a large purchase without talking to me first but he would nickel-and-dime us to death," explains Rebecca. "He loved to shop at thrift stores, finding old records to add to his collection or some item he was going to resell on eBay and make lots of money. But reselling the stuff didn't seem to be as much fun as buying it.

"I was in charge of paying the bills and buying groceries, which meant stressing over where the money was coming from and what could be paid and when. I became an expert at borrowing against one credit card to pay another. I'd sit in the grocery store parking lot checking the balance on a card so I knew how much food I could buy. A counselor once suggested we try sharing the financial responsibilities, so I had him help me pay bills that month. It was a disaster. He became foul tempered and even more difficult to live with because he was 'stressed out about our finances.' And I thought paying bills was stressful before! I never invited him to help again, and he never asked to."

Morality as a Means of Power and Control

"If I didn't agree with him on some topic, such as politics, it wasn't seen as just a difference of opinion," says Rebecca. "It was a lack of morality. If my friends liked a show he didn't approve of, I heard a lecture about the kind of people I associated with, the implication being that I, too, must be immoral if I were willing to hang out with them. I can look back now and realize how stringent and uptight and prejudiced he was but, at the time, I vacillated between seeing myself as a horrible person or being mortified and humiliated when he'd spout off his extremist views to others."

Another way that power and control is played out in unequal relationships is through the use of religion and morality. Many abusive men are quick to quote the Bible, explaining that "God intended wives to be subservient to their husbands." However, they seem to have completely skipped over the verse that describes a husband's duties to his wife. Just like any cult leader, they are able to pick and choose from religious works to suit their own interpretation of the way things ought to be.

It's a scenario Rebecca came to know firsthand. "I would get so anxious at dinner time. Our son was about 4. I made sure his napkin was on his lap, he was as close to the table as I could get him, and his plate was right up next to him. I'd remind him to lean over his plate when he ate but, inevitably, he would drop some food down the front of his shirt and Shawn would start yelling at him. If I said anything about how this was normal for a child his age, Shawn would throw his silverware down on the plate and storm out of the room. My son would ask why Daddy wasn't eating with us and if it was his fault Daddy was mad while I tried to distract him and hold back tears. I began biting my tongue rather than risk another blowup. Ten years later, I still feel guilty for the times that I desperately wanted to defend my son but didn't."

Children as a Means of Power and Control

"My son would start making comments that parroted his father. 'Mom, did you lock up the house?' Or 'You're cooking? Don't burn the house down!' He didn't mean them in the same sarcastic, demeaning way his father did, but hearing those words come out of his mouth, through his innocent smile, was a whole other kind of pain."

Another favorite tactic that many abusers find effective is using the children to manipulate and control the relationship. If the victim is not a legal immigrant, the abuser might threaten to have her deported, telling his wife she will never see her children again. If he has the only job (or just a better paying job), he'll make sure she knows he can hire a better lawyer or entice the children away from her with more expensive gifts. An abuser will undermine the authority of the other parent, treating them dismissively in front of the children and allowing the kids to do things the other parent has already forbidden.

"A wake-up call for me was the day we were heading to a friend's house and I was driving," says Rebecca. "My son told me to 'beat that car, Mommy.' I laughed and said (rather passive-aggressively, I admit) that I didn't have road rage like Daddy. Enraged, Shawn smashed the casserole dish he was holding into the dashboard, shattering it. I found myself simultaneously apologizing profusely to him and telling my son that Daddy had dropped the dish on accident and broken it. Ten minutes later, I was smiling and relating the same story to our friends as I asked for a towel to clean up the mess. All I could think was that even a kid had to know something wasn't right, that I was lying. What kind of lesson was I teaching him?"

I've often seen that it's the children who become the deciding factor in whether a victim stays or goes; but having a child doesn't make the decision any easier either way. If anything, children make it much more complicated. Victims can become petrified into inaction by questions they have no answers to. What kind of impact will a separation or divorce have on the children? What will custody and visitation look like? How will the other person treat the kids when it's their turn and their responsibility alone? Will the kids resent their healthier parent for initiating a divorce? Even in an abusive relationship, there is no simple answer when it comes to deciding whether to stay and make the best of it or get out and hopefully make a better life on their own.

Stress over a seemingly inescapable situation can manifest itself physically, too. "I suffered such intense back pain," says Rebecca. "I'd beg him to rub it at night, and he would usually comply. Surely, this was a sign of what a giving husband was? But then I realized how, on my drive home, my back was tensing up. I could feel the muscles clench and seize up as thoughts raced through my mind.

How long after 5 is it? He says it only takes 10 minutes to get home from my job. It's already 5:08. I only stayed behind a few minutes to talk with a colleague, but he's going to be mad if I admit that. 'You haven't seen your family all day! Don't they mean anything to you?' If I can hurry up and get home in the next five minutes, maybe he'll be OK."

Recognizing Abuse from the Inside Out

Many of the men and women I have met with over the years come in with one main question. "Am I being abused or am I just making too much out of this?" They begin describing their interactions with their partner and, inevitably, I confirm they're experiencing abuse. I think a part of them knew the answer but they needed to hear it from someone else. They needed it confirmed. Sometimes they even need that confirmation again and again throughout therapy.

I had a client who, upon receiving confirmation she was being verbally abused, felt she needed to give her marriage one more chance before turning to divorce. She asked me: "When will I know I've tried long enough? When will I know I'm done?" I explained to her that I couldn't give her that answer, that only she could provide it. But I did warn her that, once you realize what's going on, that it's abuse and you don't deserve it, you won't be able to stay in that situation for long. The blinders are off. You're seeing the world around you for what it really is. Maybe it's that innate desire not just to live, but to live free, to experience dignity that moves a person to finally leave. Maybe they just can't shove the memories and pain away any longer. Whatever the motivation, continuing to live in that situation soon becomes intolerable for most victims.

It can feel like coming out of a fog, like the relief after driving through a storm so intense, you've had to focus solely on the road right in front of you, and now things are starting to clear. You can see the world around you. You realize how tense you'd become as your shoulders finally start to relax and your grip on the wheel loosens and pain streaks through your stiff knuckles.

After Rebecca freed herself, as wonderful as that was, it wasn't the end of her suffering. "After we split up, I tried to hold onto a nugget of love for him," she says. "I felt like I was hiding it away in a corner of my heart, protecting the memory of the love I once had for this man, the father of my child. I wanted to be able to say 'a part of me will always love him,' but Shawn wouldn't stop harassing us. He wouldn't stop trying to hurt me, even after I was granted a protective order. As hard as I tried to hold onto that last piece of love, he killed that too. Just like when we were together, he reached past every defense and pierced the most vulnerable part of me. There's nothing left for him now. It's like that part of my heart … well, empty isn't the right word. It's like it's just dead. There's no hatred or anything that intense. Just this somber feeling of staring at a grave stone marking the place of the feelings I once had for him."

The Long Road Ahead

I often warn clients that have made the decision to get out of an abusive relationship: unfortunately, the abuse is not likely to stop when one person walks out of the door, as happened with Rebecca. Abusers are used to being in control. The victim has become their prized possession and, just like their car, the idea that they would walk outside and find that it's gone is not an acceptable situation. Abusers will call and text the victim dozens of times an hour. They will jump from one tactic to another: apologizing, blaming, being angry, pleading, making the victim feel guilty, blackmailing the victim, being angry again. I've seen some victims become so worn down, they go back simply because it's easier to handle the abuser while living with him than the tactics he resorts to when their gone.

Oftentimes, a large part of my job as a therapist is simply to be a constant reminder that what they went through really was abuse, to remind them they didn't deserve it. I work to help keep them from falling back into old patterns of minimization and denial. I cheer their accomplishments and point out their strengths and how far they've come in their healing process. Sometimes, when they look around and see all the people around them who seem to have such *normal* lives and *happy* marriages, they can become discouraged. But then I remind them of how far they've come, of the role model they are for their children, and of the future, free of fear, they now have ahead of them.

"Though he's a wonderful man and not at all like my abuser, I can't even sit outside and enjoy coffee with my new husband without fearful thoughts and triggers," Rebecca says. "I'm playing a game on my phone. Will he get angry about the 'mindless way I waste my time?' He's going inside. Does he expect me to go in, too? Will he be aggravated if I don't? It doesn't matter that those thoughts never cross his mind. They cross mine, and rational understanding of the healthiness of my current relationship just can't fully override the anxiety coursing through my body."

Survivor' Scars and Other Signs of Courage

I would like to be able to say that these brave, incredible women not only go on to live full, rich lives, but they completely leave the abuse behind them when they finally escape their abuser's influence. Unfortunately, that's not always the case. The invisible wounds leave hidden scars that may fade in time, but they usually don't go away completely. Even so, these incredible individuals—if they have done the hard work of healing—have an ability to turn their experiences into something beautiful. They're more likely to recognize abuse in others and are often the first to reach out and offer their help.

"As hard as it was to leave, I have never regretted being out of that relationship," says Rebecca. "It seemed to drag on for so long, especially leading up to the actual divorce. And it's been a slow process, rebuilding my life. I was so worried about how my son would handle not having his father in his life. Shawn wanted a package deal, so when he couldn't have me, he abandoned our son as well. But I started seeing changes in my son within six months of his father's leaving. He would fall asleep more easily and sleep through the night. He wasn't as clingy with me and started talking more. Friends and family mentioned how he was holding actual conversations with them, whereas before he would barely look at them or say a word. I found out later: my mother was afraid he might be autistic! I can laugh about it now, but it was painful, too, realizing that as hard as I was trying to protect him, he was suffering just as much as I was. But now, we're both free and so much happier."

One of the most rewarding aspects of my job as a counselor is getting to see victims rebuilding their lives, becoming survivors and, eventually, *thrivers*. Celebrating the small victories that mean so much along the path to rebuilding their lives. The college student who's able to pull her grades back up now that she's not devoting all her time and attention to a boyfriend who constantly critiques her. The single mom who's so proud of the fact that she can support her family financially and is in the process of buying her own house for the first time. Rebecca, who has created a successful career for herself and spent several years learning to enjoy single life and raising her son. He is now a carefree, gifted high school student, and she could not be more proud. A few years ago, Rebecca remarried a kind and caring man who exemplifies the character she always wanted her son to see in a husband and a father. She describes her life now as "something out of a dream. Something I never thought would be possible in real life."

There are many more abusers (and so many more victims of abuse) out there than most of us realize. Victims struggle to get through their day, trying their best to *look normal* and show everyone a mask of happiness, primarily because they don't believe other people will understand their situation. But there are also many, many survivors out there: people you know, but don't realize the hell they once lived through. Their lives will never be what they once were before the abuse. The scars they carry will never fully heal—scars inflicted by the people they chose to spend their lives with, the one person they once believed loved them more deeply than anyone else on Earth. But from this pain, and the shell of a person it created, they built a new life of independence, self-reliance, and self-worth. They filled in the hollows created by their abuser with self-respect and a demand that others treat them with respect as well. These people, these survivors—these thrivers—are some of the strongest, most courageous people you will ever meet.

About Alison Pourteau, M.A.
Licensed Professional Counselor-Supervisor

Alison holds a bachelor's degree in psychology and a master's degree in clinical psychology from Sam Houston State University (SHSU) and is now a licensed professional counselor-supervisor (LPC-S). Alison operated a non-profit counseling clinic, Brazos Valley Counseling Services (BVCS), for six years, where she trained dozens of students and interns and oversaw the provision of low-cost counseling services for low- and middle-income individuals and families.

Upon closing BVCS, Alison opened a private practice. She continues to work with a wide variety of clients, including those with bipolar disorder, depression, sexual abuse, and those in need of couples or family counseling. She contracts with Twin City Domestic Violence Services to provide counseling services to their clients, notably survivors of domestic violence. She also provides training about domestic violence to local schools and agencies.

Alison currently serves as co-chair of the Brazos County Coalition Against Domestic Violence and is a member of the Crime Victims Conference Alliance, which organizes the annual Every Victim Every Time Conference. She also volunteers her time as an expert witness in domestic violence for the Brazos District Attorney's office and other local counties.

In addition, Alison continues to supervise LPC-Interns seeking licensure. She is also an adjunct professor at Blinn College who teaches general psychology.

Work towards making your life the life you deserve. Be gentle to yourself and treat yourself to some wonderful new life experiences.

Domestic Violence Survivor

CATHY FIELDS

Three years ago I was unfamiliar with the prison process. I wasn't sure what to say to the guards. I wasn't sure what to say to the inmates. I wasn't even sure I would last because I had no idea what I was doing. I was alone in unfamiliar territory.

The buzzer sounds overhead and though I've heard it many times, it still makes me jump. The large gate inside the prison wall slides open. The grating sound sends a chill down my spine. The guard watches me as I step through. Sometimes they ask why I'm there. Other times they don't. I sign in, grab my things, and carry them with me down the long, cold hallway.

The guard escorts me down the hall. I wonder if I should be wearing a vest or some kind of protective gear. We walk past the kitchen where several men are cleaning up after dinner. I tip toed around the wet spots and mushed food on the ground to keep from slipping and dropping my things. The men stop cleaning and look up as I walk by. The guard releases a grunt that signals them to get back to work. The guard doesn't carry a gun but has an unseen power.

The guard takes me through the final gate. The door locks behind me and the sound haunts me in my sleep. A couple the inmates are trustees and dressed in blue prison uniforms. I always feel better when they're around. People in uniform are supposed to make you feel safe. But most of them are dressed in orange.

The inmates talk amongst themselves while I set up at the front table. I am surrounded by women who are guilty of theft, prostitution, drug offenses, child abuse and murder. Inside the large concrete room sits 13 inmates. Although their offenses range from misdemeanors to felonies, and some of them are awaiting trial, we all have one thing in common: we are all victims of violence.

I introduce myself and tell them why I'm there. I tell them we'll be talking about domestic violence, power and control, boundaries, and safety. The class I was there to teach is called Relationship

Awareness. Let me explain why this is so important.

My relationship started like any other. We were high school sweethearts and anxious to leave our small town behind us. It was my first serious relationship, and like many teens, I had no idea what was normal. He was leaving for the military and I was alone, sixteen, and pregnant. This unborn baby had become my life. I started reading as many child development books as I could find because I had no idea what I was doing and I was going to be alone.

He came home briefly when I was seven months and we got married. He didn't come back until the day before my induction. He was gone two weeks later. Fortunately, the baby was healthy and I was completely focused on him. I cared for him, sang to him, and talked to him every day. Eye contact during feeding was important, I had read somewhere, for bonding and forming attachments. After two weeks of staring at a baby who wouldn't stare back, I started to get depressed. It didn't take long for him to catch on. One day, he finally started staring back at me. That was a great moment for us. It was a small accomplishment but I felt like I had done something right as a mother.

Our baby was four months old and I had just turned seventeen when we got situated into base housing. I believe that building on Alabama Avenue has now been destroyed. The whole thing was made of concrete and it was cold and very gray. Although the place was awful, I remembered feeling excited. I've always been an optimistic person so I knew we would make it home. But my optimism faded as we began fighting every day. He accused me of sleeping with the cable installation guy which was absolutely ridiculous. I tried explaining that the man hadn't even come inside but that didn't matter. He stormed out and I was scared, alone with a baby, and a thousand miles from home. I wasn't excited anymore.

I decided to get a job but ended up quitting within two weeks. He said the babysitter was no good and I needed to stay home. I didn't mind staying home because I loved spending time with our son. Every day we'd play different types of games because I wanted to make sure he was developing properly. I read to him, talked to him, sang songs with him just like I had a few months earlier. Caring for my baby got me through those difficult times. Without him, I wouldn't have had a reason to live.

After a year of continued fighting, it was time to move on. He was being relocated to the south and we had planned on separating. I stayed with my parents while I was waiting on living arrangements. I started taking a few classes at the nearby community college and that gave me a reason to stay home. My parents did not know that my plan was to stay home all along. I had no idea that his plan was to get me back.

He was returning to base after a visit and got into an accident. The car had been totaled and he needed to get back to base. He asked me to bring him my car and to have my parents follow me so they could drive me back home. When the time came for the vehicle exchange, he had a change in plans. He asked me to drive him back to base and my parents offered to take the baby home. I didn't want to go because I had a feeling I knew how this was going to end. My parents had no idea what was going on between us and I was not prepared to tell them.

Two days ended up lasting a week. I stayed with a few friends of ours but it was torture. I hated being away from my baby. To make matters worse, the semester was midway through and I could not drop or withdraw from classes over the phone so I ended up with three F's on my first college transcript.

We got the baby back, found an apartment and I started a job waiting tables. I soon found a local college and began taking classes again. I always enjoyed learning and thought I might be able to make things work this time. As always, our relationship cycled and got worse.

Our Christmas party for work was held at a local school. He wasn't interested in attending so I went anyway. When I came home from the party that night, he and the baby were gone. I looked all over the apartment, went outside, started to panic, and started thinking the worst. Had something happened? Were they in the ER? Had he taken the baby from me?   He came through the door a little while later with the baby in his hands. I immediately grabbed our son from him and he was cold all over. He was wearing only a diaper and wrapped loosely in a small blanket.

At some point that evening, he decided to check up on me. He thought the party was being held at the restaurant. When he arrived and realized no one was there, he started driving around town looking for me and had taken the baby with him. I began to worry about his judgement after that.

Once I found cuts on his wrist and he claimed that it was nothing to worry about. I asked him to see a psychiatrist and he agreed. After a visit or two, he told me that the two of them had determined that I was the problem. I thought maybe he wasn't telling the truth about our relationship. Maybe he was painting me as a horrible person. Either way, I knew something horrible was coming.

We were arguing one night and I was leaning against the wall. He slowly came up to me and I thought he was going to hold me. Instead he put his hands around my throat and I started to feel pressure on the sides of my neck. I wasn't sure what he was doing but I could feel him resisting the urge to squeeze harder. He was struggling with himself but I managed to squirm away.

Another night, I was standing in the doorway of our bedroom and he was in the kitchen about three feet away. We were both upset but suddenly his demeanor changed. He slowly reached for a kitchen knife and the manner in which he grabbed it was unnerving. It was very smooth, slow, and calm.

He wanted me to take the knife. He asked me to kill him because

I was already doing it by threatening to leave. I took a few steps back into the bedroom until I plopped down on the bed. The knife was now staring me in the face. I was crying, pleading with him to stop, and to put the knife down. He saw the knife in his hands and asked if I really thought he was going to hurt me. He put it down, grabbed me, and held me close. I thought very seriously about reaching for it. I was terrified.

One night we heard noises coming from our son's bedroom. We looked in and he was playing with a few toys in the dark. The moonlight came in enough that we could see him maneuvering the toys in his little hands. When my husband flipped on the light switch our son turned and saw us looking at him. He quickly, without hesitation, ran and jumped back into his bed. I thought it was so cute and funny. I felt myself moving forward, ready to laugh and pick him up into the air but this monster yelled at him for being out of bed. I realized just then how afraid we both were.

One night I tried leaving. I grabbed my baby and attempted to walk out the back door. He stood in the doorway and begged me to stay. I went for the front door and again, he rushed in front of me and stood in the doorway. At this point we were both crying and upset. Then something happened that changed everything. I wasn't sure what was keeping me in the relationship. It may have been the Christian upbringing or my family's conservative values. Maybe I was embarrassed to go back home, a failure of a wife and mother, but something shut all of that down.

I saw the look on my baby's face as I carried him in my arms. He was frowning and looking back and forth at both of our faces. I had never seen him frown this way before. His beautiful brown eyes were filling with tears. His little fists were balled up. He was frightened and it absolutely broke my heart. I didn't want this in my child's life. He was barely two but he knew something was really wrong. We had become prisoners and were unable to leave.

He offered to leave and allowed me to stay in the apartment; so I did. I didn't realize that by staying there he knew where I was at all times. He had a key and could walk in at any time. He also had friends in the apartment complex keeping an eye on me. His name was on the lease so he was never really gone. He just wanted me to think he was.

Then he threatened to take away my baby, the most precious thing in my life. He was in the military and could afford housing and childcare. I couldn't but that wasn't going to stop me from fighting like hell. I called lawyers and shelters asking for free advice. They all said the same thing. "If you aren't a drug addict or alcoholic, no judge will take your baby from you. It doesn't matter if his job pays more, or his apartment is bigger. He's just trying to scare you." These strangers gave me the hope I needed.

"I don't want to be your wife anymore." That was the hardest thing I ever had to say but I cried and coughed up those words, not knowing what was going to happen next. It felt like something between us had been broken right at that moment. For just a moment, I was unshackled and that was my opportunity to leave. I packed my car to the top and headed back home. I couldn't take everything but I had what was most important, my baby, and no one was going to change that.

Back home I decided to file for divorce. I was the first and only person in my immediate family to divorce and felt so ashamed. My mother actually paid for it. It was difficult to serve divorce papers to a soldier who was floating somewhere out in the Atlantic. It was the longest two years of my life.

The day I left the courtroom a song on the radio played with the lyrics, "I feel like a newborn." It physically felt like a weight had been lifted from my chest. I felt liberated from that monster. He no longer had a hold over me. I had received full rights which meant no child support. I didn't know how to describe what happened between us but at that time I would have never called it 'domestic violence.'

My education was a priority so I scraped by over the next few years and managed to get my bachelor's degree. Five years later, I began a Master's program for Victim Services Management and realized that this is the work I was meant to do.

When I started having trouble in a new relationship, I felt lost. I still had no idea what a healthy relationship was. I started thinking about that 20-year-old and how she jumped into that car, piled to the top, and drove two states away to get back home. I envied that girl even though she only had $20 to her name. She was brave, daring, and willing to do whatever she needed to. Not because she was fearless but because she knew what needed to be done. A few years later, she found herself unhappy in her relationship and completely clueless.

This time was more confusing because I was a fighter. I didn't have someone coming at me with a knife. I didn't have someone put his hands around my throat. I was in an unhealthy relationship and I worried about the path in which we were headed. This time, I recognized what was happening and was able to turn things around.

Learning how to communicate was the first and most important step. My current husband has provided me with an environment in which I can grow. I feel free to make decisions. I feel free to make comments even if I know he won't like or agree with them. He is an equal partner in our relationship which is really great on cleaning days!

I have grown tremendously over the last few years. I am able to communicate how I feel, and what is healthy and unhealthy. Although it took time and years of therapy, I'm in a happy and healthy relationship. I have my own identity. I have my own friends and hobbies. My growth is supported and I have an equal partner in life. I am absolutely free and that feels powerful.

The difference this time is knowledge. I read every book I could find. I was accumulating books faster than I could read them. One of the first books I read was called *The Verbally Abusive Relationship* by Patricia Evans. She discusses how damaging verbal abuse can be. It happens behind closed doors and women are the only witness to their abuse. Her book got me thinking about men and the power and control they have over women. I thought back to how I was told I was a bad mother and would never make it on my own. It tears you apart when you start to believe it.

Then I read *Why Does He Do That* by Lundy Bancroft. Mr. Bancroft has worked with abusive men for many years and the most important lesson I learned was how different and yet similar abusive men can be. I learned how the abuser's version of events is very different than that of his victim. He discusses the myths surrounding abusive men and how society makes excuses for them while putting blame on the victim. He also mentions that as the relationship progresses, the abuser will attempt to exert more control over his victim. When and if the victim recognizes this control, and decides to resist, the abuser thinks the victim is the one who is changing. He also describes how manipulative abusive men can be which is why it's so easy to fall in love with them, stay with them, and believe them when they say they'll change. His work is brilliant and was truly an eye-opener for me.

After learning about verbal abuse and abusive men, I set out to learn more about the victim, in most cases, the woman. *Battered Wives* by Del Martin is an older book but necessary to read if you want to understand the history of the battered women's movement. I flipped through those pages enraged with the information I was learning. Her book discusses the history of violence in the family and against women. I was ready to pick up the next book.

The Battered Woman by Lenore E. Walker was so disturbing, I had to put it down for a few months before picking up and continuing where I left off. I literally cried as I read through those pages. I thought back to my old relationship and how it cycled from happiness to stress to abuse and around again full circle. I knew what these victims were going through. My empathy was out of control. I cried reading these victim stories, their last moments, and thinking about the children that would grow up without them.

Then, I started learning about how abuse can affect victims. Dr. Judith Herman wrote a book called *Trauma and Recovery: The Aftermath of Violence-From Domestic Abuse to Political Terror.* I learned about why victims stay in these relationships for so long. It helped me realize why I had stayed as long as I had. She writes about the history of the study of Posttraumatic Stress Disorder and what it does to victims. After reading her work, I became more interested in trauma. As I was learning about myself and how my experiences shaped my own life, I wanted to know how these type of experiences shaped the lives of children.

Dr. Bruce Perry wrote a book called *The Boy Who Was Raised as a Dog.* His book covers several cases he has worked as a child psychiatrist. His work discusses how trauma can affect a child's brain. Because their brain is still developing, trauma has a greater effect on them than adults. Their survival ultimately depends on the therapeutic interventions and their support system. I thought about my child and how his earlier experiences may have affected him. This book was haunting and again, I was brought to tears.

Education has become the key to getting things right in my life. Learning doesn't stop after high school, college or graduate school. It is a lifelong journey that could save you and your child's life. My son is now 16 and we have the best relationship. We discuss problems at school or with his friends. We talk about relationships and other topics like feminism, racism, and the transgender bathroom debate. He is smart, strong, and athletic. I cannot wait to see what he makes for himself. To this day and always, he will continue to be my greatest accomplishment.

I teach the inmates about different types of abuse and the physical and emotional consequences. We discuss what a healthy and unhealthy relationship looks like. We talk about communication and how to use "I" statements. Yes, they've made some bad choices and they're dealing with the consequences of them, but it's never too late to educate yourself.

The inmates and I discuss their rights in a relationship and how to communicate those rights. We discuss trauma and what it does to the brain. We talk about warning signs in a relationship and what to look for. We talk about feminism and the struggles that we have faced. Sometimes during class things get emotional. I hear their stories and although I remain strong in class, I cry on my drive home, putting myself in their shoes. I imagine saying goodbye to my baby through a glass, unable to comfort him while the guard pulls me away. I imagine the abuse they experienced in their in childhood. Sometimes I have to stop that thought process in order to preserve my sanity. It angers me, fuels me, to keep doing this work.

Once my son made a complaint about the driver's education course and how the simulator was terrible and unrealistic. I reminded him that sine he was interested in engineering, he should create something better and deliver it to the school to help every 16 year-old with this problem. He gave me blank stare. We laughed but I was somewhat serious. When you see something you're unhappy with, when you see a problem that needs fixing, and you're passionate about the outcome, be part of the solution; even if it takes years to accomplish.

I have seen, heard and experienced for myself what domestic violence can do to a woman and her family. My mission is to educate myself and others on domestic violence. I want to help any and every woman I come across in any way that I can so that they never have to experience domestic violence. In addition to the prison class, I have also taught in the local high schools and currently, in one of our healthcare community clinics.

I have worked as a case manager and driven home crying many nights because a victim I've encountered has nowhere to go. She is homeless and there is nothing I can do for her. I know trauma and I know how she got to be in that place and it breaks my heart that her children are with her experiencing it along the way. This work is so challenging when you care so deeply for others. But there are brighter days.

Once I had an inmate ask, "How do we stop this from happening to us again? How do we stop this from happening to our daughters?" My response was, "*This* is how. You're attending this class and educating yourself on domestic violence. This information does not stop with you. Share it with your family, friends, and children so they will know what a healthy relationship looks like."

I am always in the process of becoming. Brené Brown, in her book, *The Gifts of Imperfection*, discusses the need for all human beings to feel worthy of love and belonging. She stresses how we need compassion for ourselves, courage to make good decisions and connection with others to live a wholehearted life.

When women love who they are, when they trust and believe in themselves, they will realize just how valuable they are. We owe it to ourselves and our children to know our value. We determine that for ourselves. Break free from who or what's holding you back because you can. Be free and remember that *WE ARE PRICELESS!*

About Cathy Fields

Cathy Fields has been working with victims of domestic violence since 2008. She obtained a Bachelor's degree in Criminal Justice and Psychology from Sam Houston State University. She will be completing her Master's in Victim Services Management in December 2016.

Cathy works as an Employee Trainer and enjoys assisting others with their professional development. Her passion is to educate others on domestic and teen dating violence. She volunteers her training services for A&M Consolidated High School, Bryan High, Rudder High School, Single Moms Created 4 Change and Restorative Justice Ministries.

If you put in the work, you will come out a stronger, better person and break the cycle.

Domestic Violence Survivor

DEBRA COODY, D.C.

Not Choosing, Numbed My Reality

Tears rolled down my cheeks, as I silently cried so as not to awaken the man laying in the bed next to me. He is my husband. The man who is supposed to love and protect me, yet he is the one who causes me to cry myself to sleep.

It began the night that I said "I do". The change was instant! All of a sudden the loving suitor became authoritative and manipulating. That night was the beginning of a long and painful journey of mental abuse that led me to forget who I was. Losing myself worth started slowly, just one tear at a time, one word at a time that turned into twisted phrases that became a sick "not- truth" of my value as a person. The derogatory remarks directed towards me and my work began to whittle away at my self-esteem. I started becoming less of the real me and more of a robot doing what I was told to do.

Sadness weighed my heart down so much, it became overwhelming. It was caused by innuendos, accusations, and control: the suggestion that I should be embarrassed to drive a dirty vehicle around town in public, that he always had his eye on me, being told what was acceptable to wear. When the phone bill arrived he would highlight all of the numbers, going line by line, asking me to verify phone numbers he did not recognize by making me show him my address book to verify who I called. Oh, how I hated, even cringed at, an incoming call that was a wrong number or a hang-up, because of his accusations.

He was very good at manipulation to get what he wanted and nothing was off limits for that purpose. Being a submissive wife was a Christian wife's duty to her husband. He would argue this point when he made demands about the style of clothing he wanted me to wear or where I went. After we were married, he was adamant about me not going to church without him. He never wanted to go after we were married. This was a source of turmoil for me because prior to the marriage he attended with me regularly, without complaint. But after we were wed, it was not so and very seldom did we ever go to church.

A day that I recall vividly started out, like so many others, with an angry tirade that hit me hard and really hurt me. By the time I made it to the office I was sobbing so hard I would have been mortified for someone to see me in this condition. Instead of turning the sign around to open, I locked the front door and proceeded to go to the back room, where I sat in the chair crying. Desolate and alone, I was also praying to God above for answers.

Right then, I became aware of a persistent noise coming from outside the office. To my great surprise and relief, it was not a person; it was a box turtle banging itself against the bottom of the full length glass window at the front door. To me it was a sweet reminder that God was saying, loud and clear, "It is going to be all right; I am right here with you."

The turtles have always shown up at the most perfect times. During both my saddest moments and then later as a confirmation of decisions being made wisely, there they were, my encouragement. God had come up with a way that spoke volumes to my heart. He has used a turtle many times to comfort me in both the choices I have made and to remind me of his presence in my life every day.

I would ask myself, "Why don't I just leave him?" The simple answer was I didn't know what he would do to me. When there was a news report on TV about the killing of someone due to a relationship ending, he would make me sit and watch with him, then he would look me in the eyes to tell me that he understood why they had killed, and he would do the same to me if I ever left him. It amazes me how I honestly did not think that I was being abused enough to meet the standards set down by my interpretation of the Bible. For me it had required unfaithfulness or physical abuse for the breaking of a marriage vow. I had yet to realize my own inner strength and recognize that this was all very wrong. Additionally, I had not come to the understanding that there was no amount of validation that would ever make this situation acceptable.

In the last year of marriage my prayers were for others to see what was happening behind closed doors. It was at this time that I thought I was about to go crazy. Oh boy, did God answer my prayers. On two separate occasions police were called to a restaurant for disturbances. We always patronized a particular restaurant and on this particular evening, it was packed and the wait was going to be long so we ended up at a table in the bar area. The bar area was a smoking area and smoke tended to irritate him. This evening was no exception. When he walked past a husband and wife that were smoking at the bar he told them that they needed to quit. The husband said that they were celebrating an anniversary and would continue to smoke and besides they were in the smoking area. This soon turned into male chests puffed up and before long the wife was even pushed. It was a good thing that I was close behind her to keep her from falling.

Then came the police. Unfortunately, the other man had been drinking too and did not pursue the issue. Another disturbance occurred in the parking lot where there were words exchanged over who had the right to a parking space. Once again a police officer was called to assist in the matter. No ticket was issued on either occasion.

For my birthday, I decided, on my own, to have my hair cut and highlighted. When we met up to eat that evening, he was extremely angry about my hair. While sitting at the table he began with a tirade of how I did not have his permission to do anything with my hair, I should have asked him first. He was now convinced that I had a boyfriend and there were no words that I could say to change his mind. At one point I looked up to see if anyone was around close enough to hear what was being said. The couple at the table closest to us was leaving. As I sat there listening to the awful words flowing from his mouth something in me had me standing up and I left. The couple that had left earlier was waiting for me in parking lot. They had overheard and were worried about my safety. They asked if he would hurt me once I was at the house. She told me that I did not have to live in that and there where places to go for help. Still unable to choose, to change this path that I was on, I returned home.

One evening while mama and I were sitting at the dining room table, he came in from the bedroom, stood before the table and proceeded to blame my mama for our son's bad teeth. The discussion became heated and before I knew it, he was raising one of his crutches as if to strike mama. It was then that I stepped in between the two and began pushing him back, trying to persuade him to go back into the room because the police would be called if he hurt her.

Then late one night during a very loud confrontation between us, he put his hands on my face and told me to shut up. Prior to this he would only show me his muscles or make me feel them, but he had never physically touched me when he was angry. This time was different. Something deep down inside told me to calm down and take a deep breath. To wait for tomorrow and then take action.

Finally, after ten long years of living in despair, looking into the mirror, seeing that I had lost my smile, and my joy; I had to make a decision. I had just spiraled down to the bottom of a dark pit with seemingly no hope of change, I was terrified and now really mad. At that moment I made the scariest decision of my life: to leave.

While petitioning for the divorce in front of the judge, I felt strongly about having a one-year protective order. I knew that I needed this for both safety and also to keep him from pestering me. However, my lawyer refused to ask for this on my behalf because she said that would never be granted, to be happy that I had it for the three weeks. So I prayed. To the shock of my lawyer, the very last thing that the judge did before the gavel hit the desk was to add a one-year protective order to my decree. Another amazing example of God's presence when I prayed for help!

The craziness about the situation was that when I finally chose to leave I actually had visitors who came to me at work to "encourage" me to stay and work it out because that was the "right the thing to do." All of these visits were instigated by my husband who would go to the different churches in the area and speak to the preachers, explaining that I was leaving the marriage without just cause. The preachers would then call on me, one even went so far to say that It was obvious that I had done something wrong because of my strong reaction against the help that he was trying to insist upon. His help would not involve a divorce; it would consist of counseling. He was wrong. Little did he know the hours that I had spent for several years praying and receiving the confirmation that this choice was the right one. I am very blessed to have family and friends who stood behind me in my choice, and for that I am ever thankful!

That was then and now. Choices. I make them every single day. Sometimes I don't even realize that I am doing so. But nonetheless each one of those decisions have had an impact on my life! I made the choice to stay exactly where I was until I changed that choice. Because of that I am going down a different path today. The choice to leave the marriage was the best decision I made.

Why is it so easy to accept the negative judgment that someone directs toward me as a truth about my own self-worth, allowing it to take a hold of how, and what I do with my life? It is important to identify those who choose to bully, control, and manipulate for their destructive pleasures as bad influences in my life and NOT believe a single word that comes out of their mouth.

In the end, I learned that my self-worth is not dependent on someone else's opinion or approval. It is a choice to believe that God has made me wonderfully, that I am uniquely the one and only, there is not another just like me. I was put here on this earth for a purpose that only I can fulfill. One certainly cannot live life if there is no hope that we deserve it.

There is a word rattling around in my head, it is exquisitely. The Webster dictionary describes it as 1) beautiful, delicate 2) very keen. To ponder that word and then to say it in one sentence out loud "I have been exquisitely made". WOW to imagine that as a fundamental truth about myself! I will choose to believe this and live it out every day in the choices I make that will impact my life for the better.

Indecisiveness is something I struggle with regularly. Even something as simple as what to eat from a menu. I am always being the last to order. Recently though it has been easier and easier to decide. Such a trivial thing and yet I am beginning to feel empowered by even the smallest of decisions. When it came time to purchase a vehicle it was a two door jeep that caught my eye. A jeep is something I have always wanted since childhood, however, most everyone, including my mama, were not impressed by my choice. The time had come for me to stand firm for what I wanted, and stop making choices to please others.

I will continue to live this life much more fully now than ever before because, through this journey, I have learned a couple of things: 1) to accept compliments freely into my heart as they are freely given and, 2) that it is becoming fun to be decisive and making choices is liberating. It is freeing to have an opinion and to stand up for that opinion, and finally, 3) being confident in who I am. Where once criticism was the norm, now I am choosing freedom to believe and love myself as the great Creator above has designed me.

These nights when my head rests on the pillow there is continued thanks given for the peacefulness that surrounds me. Yes, the turtles still show up and put a smile on my face and a warmth in my heart that continues to inspire me to keep on living and making choices. The turtle ultimately reminds me that God is still ever-present in the mist of it all and because he is, I will continue to write my own unique story that adds color to the canvas of life and that in and of itself is invaluable! That is why I was created in the first place to live life abundantly!

About Debra Coody, D.C.

Debra Coody, D.C. is a graduate from Palmer College of Chiropractic. She has been practicing her beloved profession for over 20 years. One of her greatest joys is helping people feel better. Her favorite hobbies are gardening, fishing, and spending time with friends. She loves being creative and doing DIY projects.

It will be hard. It will be a struggle. But you are worth it.

Domestic Violence Survivor

RAQUEL MASCO

Telling My Story

Life is a series of events. We have our ups and downs. We have mind blowing moments and ho-hum ordinary days. We rise and we fall. We exist or we choose to live. We make choices and choices are made for us. We hope to have a reasonable amount of control over what happens to us. It doesn't always work out that way. Sometimes other people make choices that take away our control and our choice. In those moments our voices are silenced - even if we let out a scream or protest. When someone takes our control they take our voice. They take away our sense of security. When someone takes our control by violating our body or forcing us to do things we do not want to do - it affects us mind, body and soul. Our life is changed. How we view the world has changed. How we view ourselves can change. My view of the world and myself changed one day when I was 22, when the biggest thing in my life should have been which road to take for the future.

Let me start by saying that at 22 years old, I was living in a house (with a roommate) and I was in a leadership position role at a major retail store. I was perfect size 2 ok maybe a size 4. I was shy and introverted but I could also party with the best of them. I could hold my own. I considered myself to be strong and fiercely independent. I mean I was a single woman paying own bills, buying my own things and paying my own rent.

I lived my life without regret and no apology. I was young and having a good time was supposed to be high on my list of priorities, right? When you're young and seemingly carefree you don't expect anything to come in and derail you from the path you're on. You don't expect someone else to come along and decide to take your power and ability to choose away from you. Why would someone even consider doing that to another person? What could they possibly gain from wreaking that kind of havoc on someone else's life? I've found that when your heart is basically good you don't think along those lines. You may not always make great choices but you certainly aren't thinking about taking away another's choice.

One day someone, a man I had no prior knowledge of, decided he would take away my choice. He made the decision to interrupt and intrude on my safety, my peace...my life as I knew it. It is interesting to me that I have trouble remembering what I had for lunch yesterday but I can remember every detail of that day 20 years ago so vividly as if it is in real-time. The mind is a funny thing isn't it?

I guess I should set the stage for the day that changed my life. Remember how I mentioned about partying a lot at that age? Well, that day had been filled with it. I was with a young group of friends, hanging out at my house that I shared with my roommate. It was a mix of guys and girls. The day rolled into evening. The partying turned into casual sex between certain couples and I use that word loosely. There was a cute guy that I was with and when it was over he left my room. Our friends had brought along a new guy. I never met him before. After my cute guy left this new guy makes his way into my room. I wasn't paying much attention really as I was looking in my closet for a change of clothes. I hadn't really noticed when this new guy came in and he stood in front of my door.

He said "hey" and that he "would like to get the same thing" my cute guy got from me. I wasn't interested and said "no, I don't think so." He remained calm and proceeded to lock my door and stood in front of it. I remember the sickening feeling that rose up in me. It was a feeling of fear. I called out to my friends as calmly as I could but no one heard me. This new guy wasn't going anywhere until he got what he wanted. Nobody was going to come in my room because it was a party. He made that plain. I still wonder why I didn't scream.? Yes, he was much bigger than I was and no doubtedly stronger than I was but still, why didn't I scream? Why didn't I beat on the walls or something? When he told me to take off my clothes why didn't I scream? Did I secretly want this? No. When he took his clothes off and pulled me on the floor I felt like I blacked out a bit.

The next thing I remember is that he was on top of me, inside me, and I felt almost paralyzed. I almost threw up when he said "doesn't this feel good to you", "I'm good right", "say you like it" (in a scary voice), I nodded but I hated it. Then he said "call me daddy". I sincerely felt if I didn't say it something even worse would happen. So I said it. As I sit here writing this I wish I could take that back. However, there is no way to do that though. I wish that was the end of this story and that night. But, it was not. After he finished and left my room, I know he felt proud of himself. I stayed in my room. I was stunned at what happened but what could I say? I had just had sex - consensual sex earlier in a house with a group of people in it. What would I complain about? After several minutes one of my friends came into my room saying that one of our friends needed a ride from work. My roommate didn't want to leave and asked if the new guy would just drive her car and pick him up and if I would ride along with him. I wanted to scream at the top of my lungs, "NO", but no sound would come out. As I recount that night for this book, I wonder what was the real game plan? What was I really a part of?

Anyway, I got into the car with this person who made a choice that night to ignore mine. I remember just feeling sort of detached from it all. As we preceded to drive, this new guy takes a route I didn't recognize. He pulls into a dark place next to or behind a dumpster. He wanted me to perform oral sex on him. I was frozen with fear because of the way he said it and the way he looked at me and then that dumpster. He said "we're not going anywhere until you do it." I looked at that dumpster and all I could think was that I did not want to die there that night. I would not end up stuffed into a dumpster with garbage.

I did want he wanted and we left and picked up the friend. We drove back to my house and all I wanted to do was wash that whole night off of me. I was ashamed. I was so angry at myself. Why didn't I fight? Over the years I realized I was in shock and in self-preservation mode. The threat of violence was real and I was completely caught off guard. That night however, those thoughts were not in my vocabulary. I am not sure where I found the courage but I told one of the girls from our circle of friends about what happened the next day. She told the guys in our group who were her cousins and later on that she said they had run him out of town and he would never be coming back. She apologized and was understanding and upset with me. I felt better yet I knew I could never tell anyone else. I could never report it. After all, I was no virgin. Deep down I thought I had it coming. I deserved that because I wasn't a virgin. If I told someone I sincerely believed that everything I had ever done would be up or scrutiny. It would have been too much. So I kept that secret.

You may have noticed, as I have, that I have not named what happened to me. It is not lost on me, so here goes. I was sexually assaulted that night. No matter what I have done previously in my life, even minutes before, I was sexually assaulted. My rights were violated. My choice was taken. My voice had been silenced. This person hurt me. He took something that I was not aware would happen at the time. He took my sense of security. He stole my sense of protection. He violated me. I am overwhelmed with emotion and tears as I am truly freed from that night. It was NOT my fault! If it has happened to you, it was NOT your fault! No matter what your sexual history is, we are not to blame. Our assailants are to blame. They are the ones at fault. Oh how I hope this has helped release some precious soul from the chains of shame that leave so many of us in bondage. Shame has left many of us in hiding. We wear masks and put on fronts. We have a wall up so high and so thick we cannot even remember where it begins. It is time to release ourselves and find our true selves again. I am discovering my true self more and more every day and I have to say it is pretty damn cool. It is fabulous. I am better than just okay. Life is heading in a good and interesting direction.

These days, in my mid-40s, I have dedicated my life to empowering and encouraging other women to empower themselves. This has come after years of regaining my own dignity, self-respect and power. It was easy for me to fake these things, to put on a mask of confidence when I was really broken and lost inside. I am thankful for the day I discovered the love of Jesus. I know we all have our different belief systems but He is my rock.

In the years since the assault I have had issues with intimacy and being alone with men I didn't know and with some I did. I would have an anxiety attack if I was in an elevator alone and a man stepped into it. If you've ever had one, you know an anxiety attack is scary, embarrassing and debilitating. It's just another way we lose control. It adds insult to injury. Over the years I have learned self-awareness, triggers and ways to work through anxiety. It is not easy nor does it happen overnight so be kind to yourself if you're battling anxiety. As I survive and overcome, my passion for helping other women grows. There is comfort in true community and knowing we are not alone. As we heal forward we affect our inner world and the world around us. What a powerful sentiment - from victim to survivor to overcomer to world changer. For those of you whose wounds are still quite fresh and raw, no need to rush the process or aspire to anyone else's journey. Live your life. Walk your path. Reach for your authentic self - for better or worse. Reach for your still precious, priceless self. I am priceless. You are priceless. We are priceless. Embrace it.

About Raquel Masco

Raquel was born and raised in BCS. She is a single mom of one beautiful, now adult son, Treven. Raquel was a shy girl who loved music, singing and performing arts. She received an Associate Degree in Early Childhood Education and worked in the field for 11 years; including as a childcare center teacher and Headstart Home Visitor.

Raquel still loves performing arts. She shares this love with her local community acting in several productions: Best Christmas Pageant Ever, A Raisin in the Sun, To Kill a Mockingbird, My Fair Lady, Having Our Say: The Delaney Sisters, Doubt, and a few others. Raquel eventually directed a couple of skits and then a full length play: Crimes of the Heart.

After years of prayer and saying "somebody" really needs to do something; Raquel followed her heart and co-founded SingleMoms Created4Change, SM C4C. A faith based, grassroots, nonprofit organization dedicated to advocating for single mothers and married mothers parenting solo, who are survivors of family violence and sexual assault. SM C4C holds parenting classes approved by CPS, support groups, emergency food assistance as well as scholarships for moms wanting to continue their education, and more. The mission is to assist and empower moms to live above and beyond their own expectaions and thrive in every area of their lives.

Raquel is an active volunteer within her community. In Spring of 2016, she joined Elder Aid Board of Directors and Chairs a Human Trafficking/At Risk Youth Committee with the Brazos Valley Coalition to End Homelessness. She is also a member of Brazos County Coalition Against Domestic Violence and a couple of other community associations and alliances. Raquel is a woman of faith. A Survivor. An Overcomer. An Advocate and Activist. "I have wonderful people in my life... I am blessed."

Time will bring clarity.

Domestic Violence Survivor

KIMBERLEE A. PARMER
MS, LCDC
Licensed Professional Counselor Intern

No, I did not report it. Report? I have not told anyone. I didn't know what to do. I didn't even understand what happened to me. But I have had sex with him before. I did not want to that night. I did say no. I know better, I drank too much. It's been seven months. I cannot sleep. I am so tired. I can't breathe sometimes. I have to see him occasionally at work. Now I have to be on a committee with him.

Thirty-eight percent of sexual assault victims report significant problems with someone at work or school (1). Statistics also show that 8 out of 10 assaults occur by those we know and do not ever expect would take advantage of us (2). The mere fact that someone I have known and trusted only feeds our disbelief. We try to minimize what really happened. We play this tape in our mind that tells us this really is not what we think it is. It is even difficult to say the word, "rape". It cannot be true. That could never happen to me. Time passes and the memory/experience gets stuffed deep inside in the hopes "it will just go away". One is left feeling emotionally overwhelmed. The words "I just can't go there" confirm our decision to deny the assault. The rationale is if I don't think about it and distract my mind with other things and activities I can just put it behind me.

"Sexual assault is about exerting power over another. IT IS NOT ABOUT SEX. Sex happens to be the avenue in which the perpetrator controls his/her intended victim" (3). Also, perpetrators of sexual assault often plan their crimes. Sexual assault is not simply a sexual act where the perpetrator "loses control". Rather, sexual assault is about power and control. The perpetrator intentionally wants power over the victim. The motivation is to render the victim powerless and uses the sexual act to exert control. And alcohol is one tool the perpetrator can use to make one helpless. They may encourage their chosen target to drink, or identify an individual who is already drunk. Alcohol is not a cause of rape; it is only one of many weapons that perpetrators use (4).

A trauma has occurred. The Greek word for trauma is *tere*. It is defined as a wound or an unpleasant experience which causes abnormal stress. "Trauma is an injury that happens to us, it does not mean that there is something wrong with us or that we are bad, it means something bad happened or was done to us"(5). Whatever feelings one is experiencing is normal. The initial emotional response to a terrible event usually is followed by disbelief, shock and denial. While additional emotional responses will be discussed further on in this chapter, the immediate necessity for one who just experienced the trauma is to get to a place of safety, or familiarity. We instinctually know we need to remove ourselves from the situation as soon as possible.

Our brains recognize danger, trigger the adrenaline needed to respond and we then assess, in a moment, how to protect ourselves from additional harm. That response may be to fight, freeze or fly away (6). So we may fight, our minds may take us away to another place that removes us from that place of danger or we freeze and do nothing. Any of those responses are ok at that time. For the person being assaulted it how their brains protect them from and help them cope with danger in that moment. Our bodies are amazing. Our brains know what we need. We protect ourselves in that moment, we manage the moment as best as we can, to endure the control someone else is exerting over us during the frightening experience.

In the same essence that one knows, instinctually to seek safety, safety is also an initial and imperative goal for the helping professional, to create for the person who is seeking help from their emotional wounds. The professional will try to create a place they can come to where there is no judgement and whatever emotion or response the person who was assaulted is experiencing is normal. To that person seeking help, nothing feels "normal" anymore. They tend to feel unsafe in their bodies and in their relationships with others. Therefore, trust is a major struggle for them (7). Because fear (possibly had resulted in anxiety and/or depression), has been the overwhelming emotion for the person assaulted, the helping professional needs to meet the other where they are in their healing process and work forward from there. The metaphor of a shaken soda bottle provides a good picture of the process necessary to begin the healing needed.

Imagine you have dropped a closed bottle of soda. The inside of the bottle now has a tremendous amount of pressure. If you have experienced this event in the past and happened to open the bottle cap you learned the contents exploded all over you and the immediate area. We then learned that the safest way to release the pressure is to open and close the cap in a slow, cautious and intentional manner so as to prevent an explosion (8) There is safety in this process. The old adage of "how do you eat an elephant?", "one bite at a time" also applies. So like the soda bottle example if we release the pressure all at once we will explode. The goal is to create safety and give ourselves permission to experience our emotions a little at a time. This is manageable in small bites.

Another common experience shared when one first tells their story and seeks someone to talk to looks like, "It started when I twelve. I heard my door open again. He is coming in again. I will just pretend I'm sleeping. It won't last long, I will just let it happen and he will go away. As he gets under my covers and starts stroking my back I am aware I need to go somewhere else in my mind. I will go into my closet, or another safe place like the memory of sitting with my grandmother, or put myself on the beach again, anywhere but here. I just want the morning to come. I can get through this; it will be over soon. I need to stay still. Someone might hear. They won't believe me anyway. Plus, if I just allow him to do what he is going to do anyway, he will leave my sister alone".

For this child she does not even know what the word "rape" means. She does know it is wrong, it feels dirty, and she knows she cannot tell anyone, most likely because the perpetrator has told her not to tell with the threat of further harm to her or someone else. She has no sanctuary but possibly school or a friend's home. Her own bed is not safe. She never invites friends over. She would never want this to happen to them. She lives in a trapped world not even understanding she has a voice. She doesn't even trust someone will belief her so she says nothing.

Women come into counseling decades later and share stories of molestation since they were three years old. One woman said, "I can still smell the sweat of my 17-year old cousin". She goes on to describe, "After football practice he would come home and find me at the kitchen bar and he would drop his pants. I was just tall enough for my lips to meet his exposed genitals and he instructed me to just make believe it was a lollipop. One day my aunt came into the kitchen and saw what was happening. My aunt screamed, "What are you doing?". I got spanked. My mother never brought me back to my aunt's house again and we never talked about it –EVER!"

For these women it made perfect sense they felt overwhelmed and just wanted to" check out" for weeks, months and even years never seeking assistance. Many possibilities can contribute to the delay of seeking help. "I must have deserved this" or," I must have done something to ask for it" is a common thought some women believe. Depending on who they talk to or "well-meaning" people they may hear the same from them. If one was received by others in a negative or insensitive manner, many thoughts occur in one's mind and without the advice of safe and caring people, one remains in a place of crisis and cannot think.

Asking for help is a risk. The truth is seeking help is a courageous act in the midst of being scared to death. We must, as helping professionals, be sensitive to this reality and create the safety one needs to feel confident that when they call for help, they have made the right choice. Sexual assault is a traumatic experience that must be met with incredible empathy in order to heal.

Recovery is a must for people who have experienced trauma. It is different for everyone and an individual experience. Recovery does not necessarily mean complete freedom from post-traumatic affects but generally it is the ability to live in the present without being overwhelmed by the thoughts and feelings of the past (9). Trauma recovery is a process that occurs over time and in intentional stages. Establishing safety is the first of these stages.

Once one feels comfortable with beginning this very brave and difficult process of healing, they seem to be more able and willing to start talking about the assault and their reaction to it. This marks the beginning of the remembering and mourning phase. This task shifts to processing the trauma, putting your own words and emotions to the event and making meaning of the event so it makes sense to the person trying to heal (10). Because safety has been established one is now able to move on through this phase in a way that brings clarity to their story of the trauma rather than reacting to it in a fight, flight or freeze response. The point is not to "re-live" the danger experienced but to allow one to tell the story with no emotions attached (11). This phase is an important task one must walk through in order to process the event. It gives one the permission and time to mourn the losses associated with the trauma and gives space needed to grieve and express their emotions.

Sexual assault is not only a horrible event to experience but leaves one in a position where their sense of security is now challenged. The person is now experiencing a loss. Loss is defined as, "a state of being deprived of or of being without something we once had and now puts one in a place of uncertainty, bewilderment and renders one helpless" (12). When one feels a loss we must grieve in order to heal from the event. Recovery from an emotional loss is not an easy task. It requires one to be willing, open-minded and very brave. This is achieved by a series of intentional and small choices.

Time does not heal. Action within time does. Grief work is the process one must go through in order to deal with the loss. Grieving is one of those necessities that no one wants to go through. Many people go to great lengths to avoid this process. They avoid the grieving process in an effort to protect themselves from further heartbreak. One definition of grief is, "a conflicting mass of human emotion that we experience following any major change in our patterns or behaviors whether positive or negative" (13). Loss and grief work is not only necessary and private struggle but changes us forever. It is intense and heartbreaking. And grief work means acquiring new skills that allow us to cope with the loss. A trained professional can help teach these new skills. Once one has worked through this process then reconnection and integration can occur.

In this phase a new sense of self is created. Hope is possible now and one can start to welcome a new future. This last task allows one to redefine a new normal and then learn to open themselves up to meaningful relationships. The trauma no longer has power over them. The trauma becomes integrated into their life story but is not the only story that defines them. They can now see the impact of the event but can prepare to take concrete steps towards empowerment and self-determined living (14).

A common question asked, once one seeks help is, "why did this happen to me?". The truth is there is no rational answer to that question except for the fact that the perpetrator planned to offend to meet his/her own need. It is not your fault. Yes, it requires one to now have to process the event. Statistics show 94% of women who are raped experience post-traumatic stress disorder (PTSD) symptoms during the two weeks following the rape (15). And 30% of women report PTSD symptoms 9 months after the rape (16).

Other possible emotional responses which can occur after the trauma or post trauma, are vast. Post-traumatic stress effects one on many levels such as physical, neurological, emotional, cognitive, spiritual, behavioral, and relational. While this is not an exhaustive list it provides an idea of many symptoms including trembling, fear, crying, confusion, decreased trust, irritability, memory problems, intimacy problems, sleep disturbances, depression, anxiety, hopelessness, self-harm, increased substance use and isolation just to name a few. Self-blame and questioning one's life purpose is also common (17).

Trauma reduces a person's capacity to be self-compassionate. Recovery from trauma requires nurturing and learning the skills to do such. However, treating ourselves kindly feels odd. Cutting ourselves a break can be seen as making excuses, or encouraging self-pity. The words we speak about ourselves can be unloving and cruel. Self-hostility, just like abuse from others, impacts our ability to manage stress and can contribute to many other mental health problems (18). The relationship we have with ourselves is just as crucial to one's healing process.

Kristin Neff, a researcher and PhD at the University of Texas has conducted extensive work on the art of self-compassion. She states, "Self-compassion allows us to soften our hearts and minds in the midst of trouble and to see what can be done to change things, or to find the wisdom to accept what cannot be changed (19). It is the beginning of experiencing ourselves as worthy of kindness" (18). A person who has experienced trauma may struggle with regulating or soothing difficult emotions in everyday life which they might not associate directly to the trauma.

Learning how to regulate and manage these difficult/overwhelming emotions is one of the skills that can be taught once one seeks help. Self- soothing practices such as meditation, deep breathing, yoga, doing things that bring us peace such as walking, listening to music as well as other spiritual and cultural practices and ceremonies have been shown to be effective in soothing the nervous system (19). Perhaps the most important outcome of self-compassion is the increased capacity to care for others. Self-compassion makes us more aware of human struggles that are common to all of us. This creates empathy for the plight of others.

Sometimes we discover people who have experienced trauma find a mission through which they can continue to heal and grow, such wanting to counsel others or give back by volunteering somehow. Successful resolution of the effects of trauma is a powerful testament to the resiliency of the human spirit (20). It gives one a sense of purpose and new direction. While trauma is unfortunate, sometimes working through the grieving process opens one up to spiritual and personal growth as well as new opportunities.

An organization called RAINN, The Rape, Abuse, Incest National Network recognizes this reality and has many resources available. They are dedicated to providing appropriate and sensitive support to everyone who seeks it. RAINN knows that no two survivors have the same experience, and they strive to provide services and information that respect these differences among them as well as family members (21). Most communities have local agencies where you can seek services. RAINN can also provide the name of those resources.

Sexual violence can affect us all. Family members and friends who love are also traumatized by the person they love who has been assaulted. Loved ones may have difficulty in knowing what to say or do to help. It's okay to not have all the answers. Non-judgmental listening and simply being there can be a wonderful support for the survivor. Let your loved one know that you care, that you don't blame them, and that you believe in them. Since there is no quick fix for healing from sexual violence, so it's important to be patient with them as they process what has happened to them. In addition to finding ways to support the person you love, it's very important to take care of your own feelings. You may be alarmed by the intensity of your own feelings. It is natural for supporters to experience their own sense of shock, anger and devastation. Acknowledge the impact that this has on your own life, and seek outside support for yourself. Taking care of your needs can make it easier to provide support to others. Services are available to them as secondary survivors (22).

You are Priceless. You are worth the fight. You are precious. You are important. You do have something to offer others. That which happened to you does not define you. I know. It happened to me, too! It was painful. It was difficult to walk through. For me it was decades ago. I remember and it has no power over me. I survived and now I thrive. It is a part of my story. A very small part and a very powerful part. It is an experience I wish on no one. You will get through it. That which has occurred in my life both positive and negative has made me who I am today and I would not change any moment. I am joy-filled and remain in the present so I can absorb all that which life has to offer. I Am Priceless is the desire to want that for others.

References

1. Department of Justice, Office of Justice Programs, Bureau of Justice Statistics, Socio-emotional Impact of Violent Crime (2014).

2. Department of Justice, Office of Justice Programs, Bureau of Justice Statistics, National Crime Victimization Survey, 2010-2014 (2015).

3. https://www.colgate.edu/.../myths-and-facts-about-sexual-violence

4. Myths and Facts, Sexual Assault Prevention and Awareness Center, University of Michigan Student Life, sapac@umich.edu

5. Trauma. (n.d.). *Online Etymology Dictionary*. Retrieved July 9, 2016 from Dictionary.com website http://www.dictionary.com/browse/trauma

6. Stages of trauma recovery, March 2, 2016 / mychildwithin, http://trauma-recovery.ca/

7. Phases of Trauma Recovery, 2013, Manitoba Trauma information and Education Centre.

8. Rothschild, Babette (2010). Trauma Essentials for MakingTherapy Safer. Presentation at conference Winnipeg, Manitoba. Rousseau, C., et al, Appendix II: Post traumatic stress

9. Phases of Trauma Recovery, 2013, Manitoba Trauma information and Education Centre

10. Stages of trauma recovery, March 2, 2016 / mychildwithin, http://trauma-recovery.ca/

11. Stages of trauma recovery, March 2, 2016 / mychildwithin, http://trauma-recovery.ca/

12. The free dictionary, Collins English Dictionary, Complete and Unabridged, 12th edition 2014, Harper Collins Publishers

13. Cherry, F., James, J. (1989). The grief recovery handbook. HarperCollins Publishers, ISBN #9780060915865.

14. Stages of trauma recovery, March 2, 2016 / mychildwithin, http://trauma-recovery.ca/

15. D.S. Riggs, T. Murdock, W. Walsh, A prospective examination of post-traumatic stress disorder in rape victims. Journal of Traumatic Stress 455-475 (1992).

16. J. R. T. Davidson & E. B. Foa (Eds.) Posttraumatic Stress Disorder: DSM-IV and Beyond. American Psychiatric Press: Washington, DC. (pp. 23-36).

17. D.S. Riggs, T. Murdock, W. Walsh, A prospective examination of post-traumatic stress disorder in rape victims. Journal of Traumatic Stress 455-475 (1992).

18. Neff, K. (2011). For more information on the development of self-compassion, visit Neff and Germer's links, which also have some downloadable guided practice meditations: www.self-compassion.org. www.mindfulselfcompassion.org

19. Neff, K. (2011). For more information on the development of self-compassion, visit Neff and Germer's links, which also have some downloadable guided practice meditations: www.self-compassion.org. www.mindfulselfcompassion.org

20. Phases of Trauma Recovery, 2013, Manitoba Trauma information and Education Centre.

21. RAINN, www.rainn.org., Rape, Abuse, Incest National Network, Washington, D.C

22. Pandora's Project, www.pandys.org/secondarysurvivors (Neff, 2011). www.klinic. Centre

23. SAMHSA/CSAT Treatment Improvement Protocols, Rockville (MD): Substance Abuse and Mental Health Services Administration (US); 1993

About Kimberlee Parmer, MS, LCDC
Licensed Professional Counselor Intern

Kim Parmer is first and foremost the proud mother of three beautiful children. She is originally from Portland, Maine and married Ted, a native Texan, 28 years ago. Kim received her Bachelor's Degree from Illinois State University and her Master's from Prairie View A & M. She is a Licensed Chemical Dependency Counselor since 1988 and a Licensed Practical Counselor Intern. She is passionate about equipping those healing from emotional hurts and trauma and the devastating effects of addiction. She is a contract therapist for Shield Bearer Counseling Centers, and Career Recovery Services and Focusing Families and works part time for the Sexual Assault Resource Center in Bryan, Texas. She volunteers as a Child Advocate for CASA (Child Appointed Special Advocate) and serves on the board of Hello Hempstead, a non-profit organization serving grandmothers raising their grandchildren and helping felons returning to their community. Today she enjoys her life in Waller County attending the Journey Church and serving on the Waller ISD Board of Trustees for the past 7 years as well as the Texas Association of School Boards Employee Benefits Board.

Things do get better. Do whatever it takes, but don't go back. Learn to be happy with yourself. Realize your worth.

Domestic Violence Survivor

DANYELLE POTTER

What happens behind clothes doors in millions of homes across the world is often kept a secret. Well, that is until now. Children are being molested and raped by their own family members – mothers, fathers, sisters, brothers, aunts, uncles, cousins or even in some cases close friends to the family. According to the National Association of Adult Survivors of Child Abuse, there are over 42 million survivors of sexual abuse in America. However, that number can be far greater because it is believed that approximately 90% of sexual abuse victims never tell on their abuser (http://www.naasca.org). My name is Danyelle and I wanted to share my story in hopes of helping the world put an end to molestation and rape.

I was just a toddler when my mother's ex-husband T.W. started to molest me. I remember my mother being at work and I was upstairs in her room in a t-shirt and panties (like most parents let their two or three-year-old run around in the house). I was playing in her fingernail polish and watching wrestling. I looked up and there he was standing in the doorway. I believe he asked me did I want him to paint my nails. I cannot tell you step by step the details of what happened from there because to be honest I don't remember. I blacked it out and maybe it is for the best because I can only imagine what affects the vivid images would do to me.

The next thing I remember from my childhood is being about five or six years old waking up in the middle of the night and he was standing over me but naked with nothing but dark colored socks on. I remember telling my mother the next day and she told me I had to be dreaming. My mother told me I had to be thinking about another man she used to date who I knew nothing of at that time. She said that one day when I was about six months old she came home from work and he told her he whooped me because I peed on his hand which she left him that same night.

None of that matter to me because I knew what I saw. However, from that day on my mother would ask me from time to time had anyone touched me and if so she asked me to tell her. I remember wanting to tell her but it just wouldn't come out. I thought if she didn't believe me the first time why would she believe me now. I was 11 years old the last time T.W. molested me. Yes, by this time it included penetration. To make a long story short my abuser only spent a couple of days (if that) in jail because although my mother believed me to the point where she had the doctor check me out she was so in love with him that she wanted to believe his lies as well. My mother couldn't imagine a man that helped to take care of her parents would be hurting her daughter. In the midst of everything that was going on one weekend my mother sent me to stay with one of my older brother's godmother for the weekend. Unbeknown to my mother that exact weekend my brother's godmother (who was a foster mom) told me that I would probably be taken away from my mother and I would not be able to see her (my mother) or my brothers again.

So, a few days later when my mother asked me to tell the counselor that T.W. did not do it I did exactly what she wanted me too. Needless-to-say, my relationship with my mother changed from that day on. In fact, it was not until I was an adult that I was able to forgive her for her poor decision to believe his lies and not believing or standing by me.

My childhood as I knew it forever changed the day my mother asked me to change my story. My mother was then and forever will be my world. However, as a child I felt like she chose a man over me. I was filled with a lot of anger, hurt, and pain and it was as if I was trapped inside my own mind because I had to keep a secret in order to stay with my mother and brothers. Trust me it didn't make things better because after I recanted my story T.W. moved back in with us and would always cause more confusion between my mother and I every chance he got. I had to make a very adult decision at a very young age.

As I got older I didn't always make the right decisions. I talked back to my mother, started hanging out with older kids, and eventually ended up dropping out of high school in the 9th grade. The 8th grade teachers started passing me based upon my potential instead of me actually doing the work. My teachers knew I was smart and capable of doing the work so they just promoted me to the 10th grade. I never stepped a day in school doing what would have been my sophomore year of high school, because my mother made me go to Job Corps instead. Looking back on my life I think this was one of the best decisions my mother could have ever made for me. My mother signing me up to attend Mingo Job Corps was a gift from God in my eyes. I was able to flourish into a young lady during my stay at Mingo. The staff at Mingo played a major role in the development of the woman I am today. The Job Corps program works for those who allow it to work for them. I was able to see that there was more to life than what I had previously been exposed to at home. I was able to obtain my GED, driver license, and became one of the leaders on campus with the help of the staff. Shortly, after graduating from Mingo I returned to St. Louis and stayed there for a few years. But I wanted more out of life.

I was 21 years old when I decided to move to Texas to attend college. I was in pursuit of a better life. I sold almost everything I had from my apartment. I kept a few clothes and my car just to move into a dorm setting again. After the first semester of college, I ended up dropping out because I needed to find a place to live and a job so I could afford to keep my car. My mind was focused on surviving and my grades were affected by it. So, after the semester was over with I found myself a small efficiency to stay in and got job to take care of my financial obligations. College was always on the back of my mind and I knew one day I would return when the time was right. I just didn't know that the time would be six years later.

Even after returning to college in a non-traditional class setting I still had my fair share of obstacles to overcome. I took in my nephew after the end of his seventh grade year, was diagnosed with peritoneal cyst and had a total of 11 surgeries and two procedures, and was laid off of a job after 13 years before I was finally able to graduate from the University of Phoenix in 2013. I was determined to do what I had originally set out to do when I first moved to Texas and I knew nothing but death could keep me from accomplishing my goals.

I remember watching the Oprah show a few years ago and she was talking to men who have been convicted of molestation and/or rape and she ask one of the abusers something to the nature of "how does he feel about how he affected his victims' life?" and one of the molester/rapist said "I killed the person she could have been". I immediately thought "WOW!!!" that is so true because I knew then that the way I saw the world was not necessarily "normal". People will never understand the shame and guilt a person feels when they have been molested as a child.

Even as an adult I sometimes can feel dirty or guilty because of the things that happen to me. Embarrassed that I let this happen to me. Why didn't I speak up sooner? The guilt for letting small gifts (candy or money) keep me from talking. However, as an adult I have also started to understand the amount of brainwashing that a molester has over a child. I feel that my abuser took my innocence away. My grandmother and mother used to always tell me to wait until I got married to have sex. T.W. stripped me of that choice because he took my virginity and the sick and disgusting things he used to tell me still makes me want to gag.

I guess the biggest challenge for me was forgiving myself and letting go of all the guilt. I choose to be free and am just now starting to see the world through a different set of eyes. Today, I speak up to stop molestation. I choose to fight back by letting go of the guilt and the shame and encourage you to do the same. My hopes of sharing my story is to get more women to speak up and share their stories so we can start to put an end to molestation and rape - a plague that have been affecting families for decades. There are probably millions of people who are survivors of sexual abuse who have been keeping this a secret because they are afraid of how others will view them. I am here today to tell you that it is ok and you are not alone. We shall no longer feel a shame for something we had no control over. Let go of the guilt and release yourself from the pain. No longer shall our abusers walk around as if they have done no wrong while we are locked up in the captivity of guilt and pain. Release yourself and let your story be heard.

I truly believe that part of my calling in this world is to help others that have similar stories to mine. I have talked to several women that have been sexually abused or raped by someone or maybe even dealt with mental issues such as bipolar or post-traumatic stress disorder better known as PTSD, that seemed to feel a sense of release just by talking about their story with a complete stranger. In fact, a couple of years ago I recall going into my cell phone provider store to pay a bill and having a brief conversation about my foundation and what I was going to do with it. That conversation led into another conversation with a young lady that had been abused by her uncle and never told anyone before she spoke with me. To see the sigh of relief come over her face I knew then God had put me here for a reason.

People must learn that part of the forgiving process is talking about what has been hurting you for so long, forgiving your abuser, working through the issues that bother you the most, and learning to think with a forward mindset. Forgiving your abuser is not going to be an easy process and believe me it is not going to come overnight.

I recall receiving a friend request on Facebook from my abuser, T.W. in 2012. At first I was shocked and appalled by his friend request then immediately after I got over that stage I went into an anger and frustration based stage. My mind could not wrap around the fact that he even had the nerve to reach out to me. There I was at a point in my life where I thought I had finally put my past behind me and was months away from graduating from college and now this I thought.

To be honest and not to sugarcoat it pissed me off that T.W. would have the audacity to reach out to me. I thought how dare he! Instead of simply declining or ignoring his friend request I took this opportunity to finally tell him exactly how I felt and trust me it wasn't nice. I didn't know at the time that I wrote T.W. that almost six months to the date, God would place it on my heart to forgive him. The forgiveness process will take you through ups and downs but you have to learn to release the hatred and anger to move forward. I don't encourage everyone to have contact with their abuser because each case is different. However, you can write in a journal or talk about what happen to you with someone you trust. Forgiving your abuser or talking about the things that hurt you gives you your voice back and releases you from the silence of captivity in your mind. People must learn how to deal with their past before their past comes back and deals with them when they least expected.

A trigger is something that reminds you of your abuse. It could be something as simple as a smell, color, sound or touch to something dramatic as running into someone or something who reminds you of your abuser. It can be also as worst like actually seeing your abuser. A trigger can also cause you to go through emotional turmoil which can also be referred to as a trance where you temporarily lose your grip on reality. This can lead you into a great depression or cause you to do something that you normally wouldn't do if you were in your right state of mind; especially if caught off guard.

One thing about triggers is most of the time they come when you least expect it. There is nothing like thinking you have left the demons of your past in the past and then all of a sudden something stops you in the midst of your tracks. That can be a trigger. You must find positive coping mechanisms in which you learn ways to deal with your triggers. Some positive ways to deal with your triggers can be going to a designated happy/safe place, taking a nice long walk, talking with someone you trust, writing/journaling about what type of trigger you had and how it made you feel, or even reading the bible. One of my favorite bible scriptures that normally help me get through life tough moments is Proverbs 3:5-6. I know that I might not understand everything that has happened to me but I trust God enough to know that He has something better in store for me. Please whatever you do don't become discouraged. Know that you are not alone and God has something better planned for your life if you truly believe and do the work. You may have to get help from a counselor in order to get through this stage of life but just know that you shall be victorious in Jesus name. Know that in order to truly move on from your past you must deal with it and work on relationships that need to be mended. Sharing your story doesn't mean you cannot get over your past it simply means that you are a survivor and your voice deserves to be heard.

Reference Page

National Association of Adult Survivors of Child
Abuse. (n.d.). Retrieved from
www.naasca.org/Graphics/_ChildAbuseLives/CAlives-600x800-text.htm

About Danyelle Potter

Danyelle Potter is an accountant by degree, writer by heart, philanthropist by purpose, and an entrepreneur by design. She is also the CEO/Founder of the Forever FAT Foundation. Forever FAT stands for Forever Fighting, Achieving, & Thriving. Danyelle's foundation is a direct depiction of herself. She would like to bring awareness to rape and molestation, eating disorders, mental and rare medical illnesses while turning a negative into a positive while promoting self-love and self-respect. Her foundation will empower and encourage people to know there is life after hardships despite their dress size regardless how big or small.

There is hope! You do have options.

Domestic Violence Survivor

CAROLEE MADRON AYRES

As I sit here looking at the photographs from your funeral I see a man I never knew. I miss you. Is it possible to miss someone that was such an important part in one's life and yet caused so much pain and heartache? I wish I knew what life was like for you in your childhood. What were your dreams and interests? Thankfully, I have my extended family to share their stories about you. This soothes my heart and fills a small part of that void. There is a void that still exists, that longing that a daughter feels when a father is not the man he should be for his daughter. You were supposed to be my daddy; the man in my life that set the precedence for the future male relationships that I would have one day. You were supposed to be my role model and my safe haven; a father who loves his daughter unconditionally. What happened to you to make you do the things you did to me?

As I look at the photo I want to believe what I see. There is a tall man with a big heart. A man who would give of himself to help others. A gentle and quiet man, who was laid back and relaxed. So it appeared. Did you really mean it when years later you apologized for the abuse?

I don't recall you raising your voice in argument, however my memories are tainted and fuzzy thanks to you. Everyone that knew you spoke highly of you with such kind words. They said you were very quiet, likeable and always willing to help others. They make you sound like a wonderful person. I however, do not know the man of whom they speak, and have a completely different view.

April 23, 2016 I said goodbye to my father. His ashes were scattered at the site of the church. I was numb and emotionless. I wanted to scream and cry but nothing would come out. My husband's comforting hand held mine and I just watched as if I was looking through a glass window. It was so surreal. I was so conflicted with emotions. I wondered if the church would be swallowed with flames from the evil and sin inside your soul. I wondered if maybe, just maybe, since our last few conversations, you made things right with God. I had hoped that you sought out the direction of your uncle who pastored the church. That phone conversation I had with you stays etched in my mind. "Your uncle is a wonderful man, he never did anything wrong, he lives a godly life. The doctor said if I have another heart attack it will be a big one and I probably won't live. That's scary", you said. "I hope it's not too late for me. I did a lot of things wrong and I hope it's not too late". I encouraged you to go talk with your uncle. Tears filled my eyes and I prayed that night you would take the advice.

My earliest memories of childhood are of my elementary years. We moved to Arkansas from California, which is where I was born. I have seen many pictures from our years in California. My family consisted of my mom, dad, my older sister, and myself. We all looked so normal. Smiling, laughing, playing and doing the traditional family things like having picnics, going to the beach, and spending holidays with extended family and grandparents. I long for my brain to remind me of those happy times. Maybe it's a blessing many memories of my childhood years are absent. I'd rather think we were truly as happy as we looked in those photos.

The Arkansas years consisted of fun times with my cousins and more family times. My father and mother were hard workers. They worked at their jobs and on the land we lived on. My sister and I helped with the garden, counting cows, and watched our parents collect the hay. We had two horses, a goat, cows, and a bull that my cousins and I would chase. Again the pictures are happy ones.

It was in Arkansas that I recall the first incident of abuse. Whether this is the actual first or one of many I do not know. It's the first I remember. I do know of other incidents similar to this occasion. My memories are like a puzzle; just bits and pieces that I can't quite put together. Years later, as the truth became known, my sister and I visited with each other and together we filled in some of my blanks. It was revealed that the abuse also happened in California with her. I was under 6 years at the time.

The first incident in Arkansas was when my father decided to inappropriately touch me and he had me touch him. He showed me how to help him masturbate. He was lying on the couch; I was on his lap. We were fully clothed. He took my hand and had me stroke him. He instructed me how to do this. When he ejaculated, it squirted on my face. I turned my head as I heard him laugh. My memory fades as to what happened after that. I don't know if I cried in my room like I would imagine any child would do, or if I scrubbed my face trying to remove the ugly feeling I had. Years later I would cry and scrub my face over and again as memories returned as flash backs. I'm sure my mother and sister were in town running errands that day. When my mother returned with groceries, I told her I needed to tell her something. My father was out of the room. She busily put up the groceries and listened. My father entered and gave me "that look". I recanted my need to tell the truth. He won. I kept the truth silent inside.

Other pieces of the puzzle in the Arkansas years were of me siting in my bedroom and I would hug this huge teddy bear while I was sitting on its lap reading a book. My father was calling me to come to the living room. I was scared and told him no. I said that I didn't want to go in there. Maybe this was the same day that first incident happened. Thankfully, the teddy bear provided comfort and security at the moment.

As I mentioned before, my sister and I exchanged stories many years later. We both recall incidents where my father would masturbate in the living room while we were in the kitchen doing the dinner dishes. She recalls that I would get called to my father's bedroom and come out with coins in my hand. What took place in there I cannot recall. It's funny how the mind protects us. Years later in my adult life when I would see my father, he would occasionally give me a coffee can of change. Being a struggling single mom attending college, I gladly accepted the money. However, I felt a resistance to touch the can. There was something about it that sent a bad vibe through my soul. It wasn't until much later when my sister mentioned the coins that it made sense.

The shed in the back yard was another place of the unknown. It had a dark sense about it. Years later, as an adult I had dreams about this place. The door opened inside to the right. It was dark, very dark and small. On the left side was a shelf and some tools. Something scary happened in there. This could be the reason why, to this day, I fear small dark rooms such as restrooms. If I don't know where the light switch is to turn on quickly, I panic.

Once while at work, I was sent to retrieve supplies that were in the storage room under the staircase. There was no light and when the door was opened only a minimal amount as a source of light came in. Panic would set in and I left as quickly as possible. Thank goodness for lighted bathroom stalls to hide in. It took a while to compose myself and return to my duties.

Years later, my mother told me she saw unexplained things that now make sense since she knows what happened. In California when I was under age 5, I always wanted to be with my mom. I didn't want to stay alone with my father at home. In Arkansas, she states I wanted to stay home from school often. I complained of constant stomach aches. She even took me to the doctor. The doctor told her I had a nervous stomach and asked about any possible reasons. My mother stated no and that there were no life changes, traumas etc. She said, "She's a kid. What does she have to be nervous about?".

While in Arkansas, we lived in a mobile home. It was a nice home. To this day I feel nervous and claustrophobic entering any trailer house. The models are much different now, larger and more modern. I can tolerate being inside if there is no paneling. If there is panel siding my mind shuts down and the walls start to close in. I feel a panic arise in my throat. The need to leave quickly is great.

I feel the need to tell the good times as well as the horrible ones. This allows me to focus on something other than the bad that occurred. If all we focused on in life was the bad or negative, it would be difficult to move forward and come to a sense of peace within oneself. Here is a great memory I had. My cousins, sister and I would play outdoor games and we would catch fire flies. Our families went to the lake and we all enjoyed riding in the back of the truck. Stopping at the convenient store to get candy on the way was a special treat. It's the little things that matter the most. Cherish those moments and focus on those times that make you feel safe and loved. Hold on to that positive feeling. Don't let the darkness from your past block the light of joy in your present.

When I was in the 5th grade, my family moved to New Mexico. Our extended family lived in the area. Aunt, uncles, cousins, and grandparents were close by. We lived there for one year. There was a church around the corner from our house. I don't recall the frequency we attended but know it was enough that it impacted my heart. God was with me and I felt His presence. He was the one thing I held on to that gave me hope. That year was the beginning of my healing.

When I was 10 years old, my father entered my room one night while I was sleeping. My sister and I had separate bedrooms with a door between them. My sister says I did not like it when that door was closed and I always wanted it open. That night as I laid in bed sleeping I awoke to a deep voice. My father was repeating my name in a quiet voice. I pretended I was asleep. He asked, "Do you want to fuck?" My mind panicked as it raced with thoughts of that word. I've heard it before. I knew it wasn't good. What does it mean? Will he leave if I stay still long enough? I still am unclear what happened at that point. I have no memory of him leaving the room or any other actions.

The time frame of that event and the next were close in proximity. My mother was scheduled to go out of town to Texas to see her sister. My sister and I were to stay with my father. My best friend and I slept in the camper one evening. While telling stories, laughing and giggling, I confessed to her that I knew my father was going to hell and why. The rest of that evening is unclear. I don't recall her reaction to what I had shared with her or any questions she might have had. The next day was the beginning of my freedom. My friend's mother called my mom over to join us at her house. It was there, my mom learned of my father's abuse towards me. My mother immediately packed herself, my sister, and I and we left to go to Texas. My father stayed behind. That feeling of freedom and safety were priceless. We lived with my aunt for the Summer.

I recall my aunt asking an array of questions. Questions of what happened and details that were needed. I overheard my mother on the phone having serious conversations in a low toned voice, asking questions, her voice full of hurt and anger. I felt sad for her. I cannot recall who told me, but someone told me a counselor had told my mother, my dad could either get help or would possibly commit suicide. In my mind I wanted him gone, dead.

That summer my mother made trips back to New Mexico to take care of family business and I'm sure to see my father. Unfortunately, during this time my mother's father was killed in an accident. My mother was heartbroken. It took years for me to look at the reality of what she must have been going through. The devastating news of her husband's actions and losing the parent she was closest to must have been shattering. I am so thankful my aunt was there for our family that summer. Our lives had fallen apart.

My aunt introduced my sister and I to kids in our new home town in Texas. My sister had just made the high school cheerleading team in the town we left. It must have been so difficult for her since she was to be a freshman in high school. My mom found a house that would be our new home. I don't recall moving in. I can't recall how long we lived with my aunt. It's so frustrating to have so many gaps of time and events. What I do recall next is being told my father was coming home to live with us. I want to say we were told he had been in counseling and/or would be going to counseling. I don't remember that first encounter of seeing him. I just remember he was there again. Why would anyone allow him to come back? To be in the same house as his daughters that he molested?

Sexual abuse in the 1970s and 1980's was not something that was discussed, much less made public. Years later I was told my mother attended one counseling session when we first relocated to Texas. The session was a disaster and she refused to go back. Little did she know the enormous amount of damage that would do for the rest of the family by never returning. If she would have gone it could have made a life changing difference for me, my sister and for her. The cycle would have been broken and we would have all begun moving forward, into the healing process. Instead, we began down a path of destruction and devastation, only moving backwards. I cannot imagine the pain she endured that summer, as our world fell apart. Now as a mom, I also cannot imagine how she allowed my father to return to our home. To take the risk of her daughters' lives being traumatized and to endure more abuse.

Life resumed with normalcy as I recall. My sister and I started school, my parents worked, and family gatherings continued as usual. We attended church and I recall my father going a few times. I don't know if he attended counseling. My mother made me a keepsake box when I became an adult and inside, there were some report cards from that year, 1979. My grades were barely passing.

I had been an A/B student previously. I struggled with the reality of my father returning and surviving. To survive being in a household that I didn't feel safe in. When alone in my bedroom I listened for footsteps especially in the morning. I wouldn't get up until I knew someone other than my father was awake. The listening of footsteps became a habit that would continue throughout my early adult life.

Sometime during the next few years, my mother was working a night shift. My sister and I shared a bedroom with a queen bed. That night my father came into our room as we slept. He placed his hands under the covers trying to touch my sister and me. I awoke to my sister kicking and asking what he was doing. He made an excuse saying he was looking for a blanket then left the room. How dare he do this again! The next morning, we told my mother what happened. She made my father move out. He went to another town closer to his work. He did attend counseling this time. Although my mother asked if I wanted to go to counseling I replied no and was never taken or encouraged. Again another opportunity to move forward and change the cycle of abuse was overlooked.

Several months later my mom, sister and I made a trip to see my father. I recall a conversation with my mom about if he would come home or not. I felt it was more of a question of whether or not I wanted him to come home. I was quiet and reserved. As we entered my father's travel trailer, the weight on my shoulders increased as we got closer to him. It was almost unbearable. I saw a Bible on the table. I remember thinking that was a good sign. Sometime during that visit I was asked what I felt about him coming home. I don't recall my exact words but somewhere along the lines of "I don't care". I felt the ultimate decision was based on my response. The incredible responsibility that was put on a mere child is inconceivable. No matter what answer I gave, it was my word that influenced this important decision. I was thinking, "How can I be the one responsible for breaking up my family. Why do I feel this decision was completely mine when it should be my parents? It shouldn't even be an option! He should stay gone. I was between 11-13 years old. They were the adults! I was only a child.

The remainder of my school years remained uneventful of abusive incidents to my knowledge. My father worked out of town and was often gone for short periods of time. My mother and I argued often. She was very critical. I felt nothing I did could please her. She was unpredictable and very moody. I now feel she probably struggled to keep going, trying to maintain a functioning household and provide for her children while living with the guilt of taking back her abusive husband. Those years after my father returned were the beginning of many years of resentment and anger towards her. She had completely let me down. Years later in my adult life she apologized continuously and made every effort to make amends.

High school graduation came in 1986. I was 17 years old. My adult life had started. I was a lost soul searching for unconditional love and acceptance. Throughout most of my adult years I sought unhealthy male relationships. At the time I did not correlate them with my father's abuse. At this point in my life, I moved to Colorado to visit my cousin. I had no intention of going to college and I was certainly not staying at home. Survival was my concern which meant moving far away. I loved the majestic mountains and atmosphere. It was a peacefulness I seldom felt. After living there for a year I returned to my home state.

Throughout my adulthood I struggled. I became an unwed mother at the age of 20 and again at 30 years old. Neither of their fathers stayed to help raise their child. My two daughters gave me a love I hadn't felt before. They were my all and they gave me the courage to better myself. I was determined to provide a healthy, safe, and loving environment for them. I moved from my home town, attended college at the age of 20 and started on my career path. I worked two jobs while attending classes. Looking back, I see many blessings that crossed my path to help me on this journey of healing and accomplishing my degree. The staff where I worked on campus were encouraging and positive role models.

It was during this time period I started learning how to take care of myself. I returned to church and rekindled my relationship with God. Without him I would've been lost. I also started releasing my bottled up emotions. This lead to an overabundance of feelings. They were overwhelming. I found the courage to seek counseling for the first time. Although a step in the right direction, the counseling did not last long. The financial cost of school and providing for myself and daughter outweighed my emotional needs at the moment.

The years after college are when the flashbacks began. It was unexpected and often paralyzing. The triggers ranged from a pocket knife, a plastic piece of paper shaped in the form of a fish symbol, my hand holding something round, hair conditioner squirting from the container, blood, dreams of falling off bridges and roller coasters, and nightmares of someone trying to kill me. My reactions ranged from heightened anxiety to a breakdown where I would find myself rocking back and forth sitting on the floor. My mind and body would shut down and over a period of time the rocking would soothe away the fear. It was later throughout counseling I learned a few coping mechanisms. Having a support system to call upon in case I was unable to function, a meditation technique called grounding, and also learning how to let the memory or feeling happen. Not to fight it and go through the motions. Journaling can be a helpful tool. I also became more in tuned and was aware when these flashbacks were lurking to come out. It was exhausting. Afterwards, most of the time, I felt a sense of release and a peacefulness.

When my daughter was 6 years old she was diagnosed with a congenital heart condition requiring open heart surgery. During this stressful time and also due to having the flash backs, I made many decisions that I would later come to regret. The consequences of these choices were overwhelmingly devastating, but eventually led to a lifetime full of blessings that I will never regret and I thank God for every single day. It would be in the next few years that a relationship with a married man would catastrophically dissolve and lead to the birth of my second daughter. Thankfully my family and close friends were there to help me and my daughters through this time. I also made unwise financial decisions which led to much more stress in my life.

During my pregnancy with my second daughter we relocated to a larger town with more job opportunities. During my daughter's infancy, I became immersed with depression, and later diagnosed with PTSD. I struggled to take care of my two daughters. I was grateful to have the help of close friends and my mother who lived with us for two years. During this time, I received counseling and was able to return to work and independently provide for my family.

For 17 years I was a single parent of my two wonderful daughters. However, I later got married and have been since. I continue counseling intermittently and have learned to manage the lifelong effects of abuse. The flashbacks occasionally occur, and intimacy issues continue. Thankfully I have a patient and understanding husband.

Healing forward takes courage, discipline and a support system. It can be done and the cycle can be broken.

About Carolee Ayres

Carolee received a degree in Respiratory Therapy and has worked in the profession for 24 years. She was a single parent of two wonderful daughters for 16 years. She is now married and has a family of eight. She has served on multiple volunteer organizations throughout her children's school years. She is a woman of faith, living a life filled with God's grace and love. By being a survivor herself, she advocates for others.

Stay strong. Do not go back into the mess. There is help out here for you. Look for it, and keep looking for it. You will find it.

Domestic Violence Survivor

DIANA SOLIS

"Enough! Can you hear yourself and the excuses you are giving? You need to leave this man immediately! Today! Call the police!". These were the words my psychiatrist said to me after a couple of months of seeing her. She had realized where my relationship with Josh was heading. I already knew what I was supposed to do, but felt too weak and too responsible for him to do something about it. It's not like I hadn't tried many times before to end the relationship, but it had always ended in violence and threats to both him and myself. The fact that we lived together and that he had no real support from anyone else or means of taking care of himself, complicated things as well. I was terrified for myself, but mainly for him. "What if he tries to kill himself or me?" I asked the doctor. She replied: "if he had been serious about that, he would have done it already, and that's why you have to involve the police". In retrospect, I cannot recognize the person I had become. It's very easy to judge until you are living in a situation yourself. I did and put up with things that I never would have believed I ever would. How on Earth did I get mixed up in an abusive relationship? How did I let it go so far? Anyway, two miraculous things happened that day. First that someone spoke to me bluntly and second that I finally took action. But I'm getting ahead of myself here, so let's start at the very beginning.

I'll kickoff by sharing some personality traits of mine key to this story. I'm a typical "helper", "fixer" and codependent person. I grew up in a household ruled in part by psychiatric illnesses and the example of a codependent parent who is a "fixer" as well. I'm very empathetic, compassionate and nurturing. I genuinely feel other being's sorrow and take action whenever I can. Relationships are very important to me; I'm very loyal and trusting. Sounds very nice and altruistic on paper, but there is a very dark side to this. I have a very strong urge to be needed and basically put all of my self-worth in how much I can aid others. I tend to act impulsively based on my feelings and don't think things through, which many times leads to very inadequate choices. I have poor boundaries, which means I'm frequently taken advantage of (especially since I suppress logical thinking), easily slip into doing things for others just to be needed or feel important.

If I'm being asked to do something and I miraculously manage to say "no", it invariably is followed by an apology ("I'm sorry") or by a request of acceptance ("if it's ok with you?) and a plethora of internal guilt comes after that. It's extremely hard for me to recognize what my own needs are (except my need to be needed), or even accept that I have needs at all! If I am able to express what I want, the guilt I live with is unbearable. I feel the obligation to give it all, but feel extremely uncomfortable when it's my time to receive. The peculiar side to this, is that I am possessive and manipulative when I don't feel appreciated for "self-sacrificing" myself for others. I recognize I impose myself in this way in the first place. So in summary I want to be the indispensable provider, secretly want to feel recognized and appreciated for it, but feel guilty if I am because I must not have needs. I feel uncomfortable receiving, but angry if I don't. I'm extremely embarrassed to admit all this, but being able to realize all this about myself has been the first step for improvement.

Ok, now I'll sail towards our main story! I worked for many years in the oil industry as a laboratory technician doing offshore exploration. It's very demanding work, with schedules to where we work for 13-16 hours daily, seven days a week, for weeks or months at a time. This type of job can be very isolating and harsh, especially for a woman. The crew consisted of about 30 people and half the time there were only two women onboard the vessel. On the vessel I was on, I was the only female there. Even if there was another woman on board, I would see her an average of 10 minutes every 12 hours, because we ran 24hr operations and she'd have the opposite lab shift. Our interaction consisted of our toolbox meetings with each shift change.

Crew members have very little stimulus and a lot of stress. It can feel like being incarcerated at times. Now, with this man/woman ratio, you can imagine the girls get a lot of attention they don't want or ask for. We learn pretty quickly that it's very hard to be friendly without your intentions being misinterpreted for something else. I also inherited my mother's pretty and voluptuous genes, which has felt like a blessing and a curse. I've struggled with resenting and liking my beauty all of my life, especially since I was molested for a year at the age of thirteen and, as most victims of sexual abuse do, I blamed myself for that. During my offshore jobs, I would spend my time either working in the lab or confined in my room, avoiding unnecessary interaction for the most part. Even so, some sexual harassment at the vessel was a reality. There were a myriad of stares and countless inappropriate comments. On one occasion I found a drawing of what someone imagined I looked like naked in my lab.

One offshore job in particular stands out in my memory. It was a long project and I knew I'd probably be there a couple of months. Most of the crew I didn't know and one man in particular, Josh, acted especially charming from the very beginning. He worked as a deck man on my shift, but also came and helped me in the lab each time he could, which was not part of his duties. However, I appreciated it very much. We started flirting and then "dating", if you can call it that when you are working on a ship. Several reliable people told me he was "bad news" and not to be trusted, but I didn't listen. Early on he started displaying a lot of possessiveness and wanted to make it very clear to all other males onboard, that I belonged to him, sometimes in quite embarrassing forms. Along with this, it didn't take long for me to realize that we barely had anything in common. This was the beginning of the worst roller coaster ride of my life and an extreme and nightmarish version of trying to end a relationship with someone you work with! Within a two-month period in the vessel, I tried to break up with him three times, but he was very persistent and of course I couldn't get away from him! This situation coupled with my loneliness would make me cave into getting back together with him. He was my closest friend there.

That job with Josh lasted almost three months. He was supposed to go back temporarily to his parent's house at the time the job ended and then move in with a friend. Unexpectedly, his friend decided to get a different roommate. Josh's parents told him he could not stay with them, because his dog was pregnant and was supposed to deliver a large litter of pups. They didn't want to deal with the pups. He told me he didn't have any place to go. I didn't want him to be homeless, especially because of the dogs. Furthermore, I only knew him for three months, and I never lived with a man before and wasn't comfortable with the rocky relationship at all. Again, I made the mistake of not thinking things through and I told him he could move in with me. I had to help him move out and make the long 8hr drive with a large moving truck from his hometown to mine. After a particular argument on that drive, I distinctly remember thinking that I had made a huge mistake.

Josh was let go from the offshore company where we worked, due to a serious mistake he made. One of them involved the serious injury of one fellow crewman due to his negligence. Once he was living with me he felt in control. Josh flipped a switch. He proved to be extremely lazy and became very manipulative. We struggled financially because he made mediocre efforts to find a job and he was not considerate of my money either. Having his dog and the eight puppies was a huge blessing, but a big financial strain also. Even after the pups were gone, I had a hard time supporting both of us. My salary wasn't enough and I had to use some of my savings every single month, which he was aware of. This didn't stop him from being very demanding of the quality of our meals or how much we went out. I remember one incident at a grocery store, where I told him I couldn't afford so much meat for each meal. He proceeded to scream at me and made a huge scene in front of everyone. As usual, I ended up apologizing to him just to calm him down and caved to his requests.

At that time, I had the misconception that in a truly abusive relationship things were always violent and nasty. Later on, after things were truly over, I learned there is a cycle of abuse in most of these relationships, composed of three stages:

In the first stage, tension builds up. I could see Josh start to act moodier and be more negative. He relished playing the victim. For a large part of our relationship he didn't have a job; he'd stay in the house watching TV all day. When I got home from work, all he wanted to do was go out, but I'd be exhausted and also concerned about spending money we didn't have. Dealing with my own frustrations was very hard too. It was near impossible for me not to nag him about his job situation, because I was so stressed about our finances. He would proceed to complain constantly about how frustrating his life was and everything he wasn't happy about, including me. Often he would rant about not being pleased with my physical appearance, that I wasn't thin enough (and I was a size 4), toned enough or good enough. All the while he was about 50lb overweight and had an extremely unhealthy lifestyle. To make matters worse, Josh had been cheated on repeatedly in previous relationships and developed an unfounded paranoid jealousy with me. He also told me I was his only "friend", so he wanted me to spend every waking hour with him. My way of trying to handle him was doing my best to calm him down and becoming very submissive. I grew a pretty thick skin to protect myself from his remarks. I knew if I reacted to them it would be far worse anyway.

Besides him, I had no life really. I had withdrawn from my friends and family.

The second stage would involve a violent explosion of some sort. He would punch or throw things. There was a lot of screaming, badgering, name calling and so forth. I have a temper myself, but I learned to keep the volume down. I knew if I raised my voice things would escalate quickly. I would try to reason with him and calm him down, and I would always take the blame. I was raised in a home where there was no yelling, my parents always got along very well; so I was very distraught and confused by the situation. Of course, over time, this stage would become more violent. What would set it off more was unpredictable. There was no set of rules to follow to avoid it. I felt like I was perpetually walking on eggshells.

Stage three is the honeymoon phase. Josh would be full of remorse, excuses, apologies and had determination to change. He'd blame his life, the abuse and lack of love he felt in his childhood. I'd listen, empathize and fantasize it would never happen again. As time went by, this stage became shorter and shorter. Things would be fun and loving, until inevitably stage one would start to brew again.

I remember very clearly the first time I realized just how manipulative Josh was. He pretended he was spending the weekend with his best friend, Tom. I thought it was odd that Josh insisted on me not going out to greet Tom when he arrived to pick him up. Later that week I happened to talk to Tom, and found out he hadn't met up with Josh at all. Through a little investigation it surfaced that it was his ex that he spent the weekend with. I was infuriated, called him and broke up with him. When I got home, I saw him sleeping in my spare bedroom and then saw on the bathroom floor one large bottle of aspirin and another of ibuprofen, both empty! I went to check on him and he would not wake up. I called 911 and they sent an ambulance. Later on, Josh told me he had taken enough of the pills to knock himself out and flushed the rest. Of course he left the empty bottles on the floor, just to make me think he had attempted suicide. At the hospital I ran into the ex. We had a talk and she said they had no sexual interaction that weekend. He was just using her to get some errands done, since he didn't have a car. That night, his mother told me over the phone that he'd used suicide threats and phony attempts to manipulate them before. His stepfather was so mad at him that he told Josh "next time you attempt suicide, don't fail". I could understand their anger, but their reaction was very harsh and knowing that he had no support from his family put more pressure on me. After that fiasco, he promised to start school, get psychological help and medication, if I promised to give him another chance. I told myself that at least he hadn't cheated on me. How could I just cold heartedly throw him out in the streets?

The following Christmas Josh and I went to my home country, Costa Rica, to spend the holidays with my family. We were on one of our honeymoon phases and had a good time for the most part. As a biologist, my biggest passion is exploring the outdoors. I love walking and camping in the area that are less visited and crowded. Those are the areas that will be undisturbed and pristine.

On my excursions I'm used to doing some serious hiking. Often times I am carrying a big and heavy backpack. Everything was well on my voyage with Josh until we took a trip with my father to my favorite volcano. Josh complained the entire time we hiked! He griped about the rain, moaned about the slippery terrain, constantly asked how much longer till we were done and whined about how heavy the two 500mL water bottles he was carrying were. I ended up taking the little load he was carrying just to shut him up. All we did was about a 3 mile walk and we had to quit after that because he refused to move another foot. My father was clearly astounded at his attitude. When we got home that night I broke out crying. I thought I was resigned to living the rest of my life with someone that didn't share my passions; I buried my need for adventure with nature. My father, who shares the same love for the outdoors, told me that he could not understand why I was with Josh, who was the polar opposite of me. Josh only had love for the busy city life and partying! I didn't have the heart to be honest with him at that moment.

Months passed and the relationship just got worse. I was driving on the way back from a trip to Houston with him and for some reason we got in a really heated argument. I became hysterical and screamed I could not take it anymore and that I wanted to end it! Big mistake to have done it there! We were on a four-lane highway, doing 65mi/h. He told me that his life meant nothing without me. He proceeded to take his seat belt off, open the car door and attempted to jump out. I leaned over to grab him and lost control of the car, which swerved two whole lanes to the right! It was a miracle we did not both get killed. After that I resigned myself to having to stay in the relationship. I didn't think I could handle someone's suicide on my conscience. I took it upon myself to make it be the best it could be. I was constantly fighting for peace, but on the way I was getting very depressed and felt my spirit dull. I started having tachycardia problems, uncontrolled nausea and fainting spells from the stress. That's about the time I started seeing the psychiatrist and taking depression and anxiety medication.

Sometime later I started a self-defense class with the wonderful Regina Rowley. Knowing how to defend myself was very empowering, since my size or the size of my attacker did not matter, it was all about technique. Regina honored and shared the experience of victims and survivors and I started to find my own voice. I understood I wasn't as helpless as I thought I was. We were taught effective physical procedures and concrete steps to be safer, while also covering the emotional aspects of self-defense. This aided in my healing process and made me want to regain control over my life. I remember for the first time fantasizing about the possibility of being able to leave him, although I wasn't sure I could still. Despite this I did tell one of my classmates and dearest friends, who was familiar with the dynamics of my relationship, that if Josh ever got physically violent with me then that would be the end for sure. So far, he'd yelled, threatened, punched and thrown things, but he never touched me. That was soon about to change and it happened the day the psychiatrist told me I had to leave him.

That night Josh told me he wanted some beer. He got two six packs at the gas station and proceeded to get drunk at our place. It was a weeknight and I told him that I didn't want a partner that drank so much. I could not allow a man like that to be the father of my children, because of the terrible example he'd be setting. It had been a very long time since I'd attempted to break up and I guess he heard in my voice how determined I was.

We had never had a bad fight with him being drunk and his violence escalated to a level I'd never seen before. He took my cell phone and smashed it against the wall, leaving a hole with a 5inch diameter on it. I tried to leave the room we were in, but he caught me and threw me to the floor. Each time I got up, he'd savagely do the same. Then he cornered me in the bathroom, put his face in my face, clenched one fist and with the other hand signaled to his cheek and said to me: "punch me, you know you want to!". I froze and at the same time realized that he wanted me to hit him so he could have the excuse to beat me to a pulp. I thought to myself that if I touched him, he would kill me! I managed to run to the main door; however, he caught me and brutally threw me to the floor a couple more times. My screams for help caught the attention of the neighbors, who called the police for me.

Josh backed off and I managed to leave the house. He chased after me and I managed to run a circle and get back into the house before he did. He started hitting the door so hard that he destroyed the frame and broke in, but again I managed to get out of the house.

The police arrived a shortly and he jumped the back fence to escape. Later they caught him and took him to jail. I called my landowner that graciously came at 1am to fix the door, so I could lock it. I was finally alone in my apartment, very bruised and with a broken soul, but alone. I went to bed, when an unexpected call startled me. It was my father. He and I have always had an amazing connection. On two occasions in which I've been severely distraught, he's called me out of the blue just because he had the hunch that something was terribly wrong. That night was one of those times. I cried like I never have cried in my life. Two days later, he had flown from Costa Rica to Houston to help pick up the pieces of what was left of me. I finally told him the entire story with no reservations. He shared my heartbreak.

I wish I could say that that was the last time I talked to Josh, but I'd be lying. My dad helped me find him a place and get him settled in, so that I would not feel guilty of throwing him out (like what he had done was not reason enough!). My father stayed with me about one month, which was as long as he could, and left terrified at the possibility of me getting back together with Josh. Josh and I still talked and got involved some, until four months later I decided that enough was enough. The funny and sad thing is that I didn't even do it for myself, but because I knew the pain it would cause my family. So even though I didn't love myself sufficiently at the time, I found my family's care for me reason enough. I told him I would not answer another one of his calls or texts and would enforce the restraining order. For once, I kept my promise, although it took an entire year before he got tired of calling and sending me texts.

My healing process has taken many years and I know I have a lot of work still to do. After Josh I found a man that lovingly helped me rebuild myself. He has been very strong and patient. Whereas I have been very unpredictable, moody and depressive. Any disagreement made me feel like I was going to be sexually or physically assaulted and unconsciously I kept testing him, expecting him to hurt me in a rage. I remember the hurt in his eyes when I finally admitted that I was expecting him to be violent towards me. Now I finally believe that he never will and that God finally sent me an angel. He loves naturally. He is smart, funny, sweet and is a wonderful and caring son, which says a lot about him as a man. We got married a couple of months ago and I can finally say that I am ready to live happily ever after and help empower those who feel they are too weak or too stuck to make a change. Anybody and everybody can save their own lives, but the thing is, no one can do it for them. You just have to make up your mind and find help. Find someone that will tell you: "Enough! Can you hear yourself and the excuses you are giving? You need to leave this man immediately! Today! Call the police!".

About Diana Solis

Diana Solis is a native of Costa Rica who came to the USA in 2007 to obtain her master's degree in stress physiology at Southeastern Louisiana University. Prior to that, she earned her undergraduate degree in biology in Costa Rica. Her main interest lies in conservation and she has worked in projects with sea turtle nesting for several nesting seasons along the Pacific coast in her homeland. She has also performed amphibian research and has worked as a marine mammal observer for safeguarding whales and dolphin populations during geological surveys conducted as part of oil and gas exploratory operations. Being a nature lover, she recently received her certification as a Texas Master Naturalist and spends time at various nature preserves engaging in volunteer work to promote conservation activities.

Diana has also as a hobby studies anthropology and neurobiology, with a particular interest in human psychology and how evolution and biochemistry of the brain shape human behavior. She also loves studying ancient civilizations, particularly the accomplishments and rise and fall of the Roman empire and the formation of the Greek city states and their contributions to the formation of western civilization.

Begin to identify things you love about yourself, and grow that list daily.

Domestic Violence Survivor

REGINA ROWLEY

#HealingForward, My Discoveries and Recovery

#HealingForward and living is my legacy. It is for myself, my mom and the countless women who have suffered at the hand of an abuser. Women who lacked facts or empowerment to take action and create a new reality. It is unfortunate how often a woman feels obligated to keep her wedding vows, when her husband doesn't keep his. They both took part in the vows; his included to cherish and protect her. May my discoveries inspire your own recovery and #HealingForward.

Out of the blue my world turned upside down when I was virtually contacted by ghosts of yesteryear. My dad had a long-term mistress. She had children from a previous relationship and then a child with my dad. I wrestled with my reaction to this virtual contact. It was so intense and confusing. This woman was an emotional abuser without reservation.

There came a point in time many years ago when I felt relinquished from any need to remain in communication with my dad. Reconciliation and acknowledgment of his wrong doing were not to be. So for my own wellbeing I forgave and moved on, wanting closure. While forgiveness should be a mutual endeavor, I have learned abusers seldom offer any words of regret, acknowledgement of wrong doing or apology. They are irresponsible, pass blame, ruthlessly mistreat their children and have no shame, only self-justification.

Generational abuse is wide spread and has left a horrible legacy of shame, with piles of skeletons in closets collecting silent cobwebs. Our world is filled with high-functioning abused individuals. Many of them still suffer with depression, substance abuse, chronic illness, broken relationships, obesity, and more. In my opinion, one of the most difficult struggles is feeling guilt or dread toward their parents. You don't just leave it behind like outgrowing a fear of monsters.

There was a time when the following thoughts were how I handled issues of yesteryear. 'Forget and move on.' 'Don't dwell on it, or let it control you.' 'Put it in the past, leave it there.' However, at this point in time those thoughts no longer worked for me. They were simply inadequate bandages covering a gaping wound; one which had been festering for decades.

Now, I realize these were archaic responses from well meaning, but uneducated sources. The reality was these thoughts only served to keep me in turmoil, held hostage to my past, and so others would not be comfortable around me. By finally seeing a counselor, I began to sort fact from fallacy, recognizing internal conflicts and moving out from the closet of shame.

By the second visit with my counselor we were visiting the reasons for my unraveling emotional state in response to the virtual touch from ghosts of yesteryear. We explored where in my body I felt the emotion and when. Were there any associations? My discoveries: I feel shut down, as though my feelings aren't important. Additionally, I felt I'm unable to advocate for myself. All of these manifested in my body as tightness and pain in my chest. To this day, I struggle emotionally and physically when I perceive I have been unheard, misunderstood and/or taken advantage of.

According to www.domesticshelters.org 88% of women in DV shelters live with PTSD. Many women are living with debilitating after-effects such as social isolation and low self-esteem. It is estimated at least 75% suffer from severe anxiety. These symptoms typically last at least a month. They can occur directly after the trauma, or be delayed and begin 6-12 months or 20 years after abuse ends. It was eye-opening for me to realize symptoms may be delayed for many years.

Journaling was suggested by my counselor as a means of releasing unspoken thoughts and feelings. It has proven valuable as a release and as a tool of discovery for my recovery. My entries tell my story.

July 4, 2015

The day of independence here in the United States of America; freedom from tyranny and oppression. The opportunity to release and let go of a past which has held me hostage for so many decades.

As I sit on the back patio preparing to write my first letter to my child self, I am listening to a mockingbird sing her glorious melodies. I'm practicing being in the moment, in tune with my surroundings, and drawing myself toward meditation. My alluring, blue wind chime dongs softly and unexpectedly on this quiet morning. A mourning dove coos in the distance... someone is mowing...

Phoebe, my devoted 'baby girl', is on her perch just inside the patio door providing unconditional love and constant support. Animals can provide important emotional support and loving devotion as we #HealForward.

Bringing my awareness to my body I acknowledge the constant tension in the base of my skull, neck, jaw, between my shoulders, and the aggressive ache in my lower back. Both of my knees have complained and lacked strength for weeks. Today there is a gripping tension between my brows and heaviness in my chest.

It seems to me I have taken such a long time to reach this point in my #HealingForward journey. Reading *Toxic Parents* by Susan Forward Ph.D. with Craig Buck, opened my awareness to the value and benefit of writing letters. My counselor confirmed this and encouraged me to begin by writing to my 10-12-year-old self. A surprising experience this week opened me up for this letter.

I attended a hot yoga class as an instructor observer earlier this week. As the class settled into Savasana I lied on my mat to relax and meditate. I began reminding myself to 'release', 'let it go' and quiet my mind. Without warning I found myself releasing the injured, inner child and her unspoken and unacknowledged fears; breaking the silence while giving my inner child assurance and a voice. Tears trickled as my body melted into my mat and the unspoken, but lived, message 'You don't matter', 'Your feelings aren't important' floated to the surface and I could replace them with, 'I do matter.' 'I do have a voice.' 'I will protect you.'.

Yoga has been such an unexpected piece of my #HealingForward journey. It continues to help me know myself completely and be at peace in myself. I have embraced and incorporated yoga classes to release tension, control my scattered and often turbulent thoughts. The surprise for me is the emotional healing impact. How amazing to me, one who had not embraced the spiritual teachings of yoga, to experience this awareness and freedom of my emotions and energies.

I want to find peace and a greater depth in uniting this inner peace with a voice, advocating for freedom from my past. So, here goes...

{Regina, you were just a child. A meek, insecure, and obedient child. You longed for peace of mind, security, liberty to speak honestly, unconditional love and acceptance. You grew up in an environment which took away your voice or the opportunity to live authentically. You were constantly told, 'Honor your elders.' 'Stop crying before I give you something to cry about.' 'Do as your told.' 'Don't talk back.'

You felt like you were unimportant as a child; your feelings weren't honored. Having been groomed to fit a mold and to not question authority, you endured years of emotional and mental abuse. There was little to no example of empathy. The depth of damage has gone unrecognized for decades. Today I your adult self, advocate for you. I want you to know *you are important* and *your feelings do matter!*

Inner Child, you can let go of the limiting beliefs, the destructive prophecies and debilitating energies of your childhood. Even though you felt all alone and were too apprehensive as a child to speak up; you are not alone. I am giving a courageous voice to your experiences. Together, we are bold, we are brave, and we are helping others find their voice.

By writing this letter to you, you are no longer invisible. I acknowledge you and set you free.

For years, since my adult taekwondo days, I have been uncovering fears and learning to break free. The past year has brought my awareness to the realization that I was still hostage, a prisoner, to many beliefs entangled and bound under the emotional anxiety of a 12-year-old child. Negative thoughts voiced by your dad, 'Watch your weight, take care of yourself or nobody will want you.', still haunt you. In recent weeks with the virtual touches from the ghosts of yesteryear exposed, an unhealed emotional thread and wounds never before acknowledged was exposed. Recognizing as an adult how I was spiraling into depression and disengaging from society, I sought professional counseling.

Among the many unquestioned myths and intimidating fallacies, the spoken expectation for you was perfectionism. Your dad's constant nitpicking and faultfinding left you insecure in your ability to think outside the box. As a child your A,B report card was never good enough. B's should have been A's and A's should have been A+. You were diluted with the mixed message from your dad, 'achieve greatness, but don't be better than me.'

Inner Child you have struggled with PTSD anxieties and a disorganized mind throughout your life. Never knowing you were enduring traumatic after effects, you chastised yourself and anguished over your shortcomings. Your childhood has had a direct impact on your adult struggles; it wasn't that you were less of a person. By advocating and speaking up I promise to give voice; to ensure we overcome your feelings of inadequacy.

Inner Child, you are important, you are seen, you matter, and you have a voice. Regina, nothing that happened to you was your fault. Like every child, you deserved a healthy and happy home. The adults in your life were screwed up and unwilling to acknowledge their need for help. Your dad was a bully. He built himself up by knocking you down. Your mom was a product of her own childhood, your dad's grooming and society's teachings to be submissive at all costs did the best she could. What self-esteem and self-confidence she may have had, was belittled and nitpicked away. She loved you, but merely existed through much of your childhood.

It was common in your childhood, and still comes up as an adult, for you to question your ability to do something new. Confidence in yourself and your mind/memory skills, was elusive because making mistakes would bring a barrage of self-destructive thoughts. By embracing and practicing this anguishing mental blame game, you are in control, instead of someone else. (Never mind this unreasonable reasoning. It has been your way of coping.)

What you don't realize Inner Child is you are allowing this negative, self-destructive behavior to hold you hostage. It is debilitating. It keeps you from achieving your goals. This is not the legacy you want for your children. Make preparation and practice a part of all new skills you want to develop. This will give you confidence and the tools to counter those self-defeating thoughts when they surface.

Inner Child, I am creating a new reality for you. I will attract and embrace the existence you longed for. Each time I replace negative, defeating, and destructive thoughts with positive, healing, accepting, encouraging thoughts, I am honoring you.

By sexually abusing you, both of your abusers expected you to deal with adult issues. They burdened you with situations you couldn't understand, control or handle. They violated your body and mind through emotional control. You were robbed of your childhood.

Skeletons of shame have lurked in the closet of your soul. So much fear. So much unknown. So much unspoken. The silence and anguish of your childhood drained your energy. I assure you Inner Child, I Am Xena. As your princess warrior I aspire to inspire societal change before I expire. No More Silence! You are worth protecting, always have been; and I will protect you. I am a force to be reckoned with.}

From my child self to my adult self.

{Adult Regina, thank you for being my Xena. I have been so tired. A variety of health challenges have added to my fatigue. As a child, I tried so hard to measure up and to fulfill everyone else's expectations. The years became decades and I am weak, weary and exhausted from standing strong in the face of so many challenges.

Silent tears streamed down her cheeks as Inner Child releases her pent up emotions. Adult Regina tenderly reminds her struggling Inner Child, 'It's okay. Take your time.' 'You have a voice. You do matter. Speak freely child. I love and accept you unconditionally.'

Adult Regina, for a number of years now, you have been advocating for me. You didn't know each time you enlightened or empowered women to be their first line of defense, you were helping me crawl out from the rocks of inadequacy....

As the inner child's thoughts stagger and withdraw, adult Regina encourages her; 'It's okay Inner Child. What other rocks have bruised you and knocked you down?' a long, silent pause. 'Where are you child? Listen to the ocean waves and birds from the app. on your phone. Allow yourself to relax Regina. Come and meet me at our happy place. I long to hear from you.'

Inner child to adult; I don't feel safe or at peace. Please keep advocating for yourself. Every time you do, I find strength and I know others do too. Women are beaten down, weak and confused. Their children, just like me, are suffering in silence. Day after day they put on a smile and live a facade. Continue your #HealingForward journey Regina and find peace; for me and for you. Nothing that happened in the past was your fault. Yet, you and only you, have the ability to find peace and hope by exposing the skeletons, speaking up versus staying silent; like I had to in order to survive.

Thank you for being my friend and advocate. You are an inspiration to other 'inner child' adults. They see your strong demeanor and draw unspoken strength from you. May you see yourself as strong and victorious. Leave complaining, about anything, behind. Leave blaming anyone or any condition by the wayside when it surfaces. Complaining and blaming are a part of victimhood and have not served me, or you, well. Regina, you are the embodiment of strength, victorious confidence and a deep, unshakeable inner peace. Embrace it! It is by no accident, your message for women is everything I need to hear every time you say it. I remind you: 'You are Beautiful. You are confident and strong. You are worth protecting.' These are not empty words to be thrown around haphazardly. They are deep and life changing because you own them, they are your story, and you share them with such passion.}

Jill Bolte Taylor, *My Stroke of Insight: A Brain Scientist's Personal Journey,* has a quote about children and emotions. He points out, they both heal when they are heard and validated..... We need to be heard and validated.

August 2015

{I am at the Miami Smartsafe boot camp for an instructor's refresher course. We were watching a new video, the story of Amanda Berry and Gina DeJesus. In short, they were kidnapped and held hostage for 10 years. One of them gave birth to a daughter while in captivity. Eventually they were able to escape. The story in print: *The Lost Girls* by John Glatt.

They had been conditioned to remain subdued. Conditioned to a specific response, that of victimhood, without hope, and without strength. I became emotionally overwhelmed and realized the correlation to my own life. How many years I lived the victim life within my own family. This video has shaken me to the core. My emotions are even more raw than I realized and I had to step away from the class. Grabbing my binder and pen, I slipped away to journal, explore and release the overwhelm. Tears trickled, and my heart heaved with the awareness and surrendering to previously unacknowledged pain. As I begin regaining composure, I once again reminded myself: I am good enough. I am beautiful. I am confident. I am strong. I am worth protecting. I am Xena!

How thankful I am to have found Smartsafe. It is a critical piece of my emotional healing and while this moment of boot camp is emotionally overwhelming, I rise above the challenge. I am Xena.

*Like a young elephant is chained and conditioned to not resist. Like the 10 year survivors: Amanda and Gina, I was disempowered through mental and emotional restraint and abuse.}

August 8, 2015

The song *Stand* by Rascal Flatts is on my mind. It has been a personal fight song through the years. Often, I feel like a candle in a hurricane, hopelessly trying to shine. Sometimes I feel helpless and as though no one understands; and I do break. Then, I become angry, I dig deeper for strength, for more courage and find another small piece of me... and I stand one more time. This is how I continue #HealingForward, getting up one more time than I fall down.

It is a perfectly splendid morning on Singer Island beach. I'm reminded of a quote by Isak Dinesen. He declares salt water is the cure for anything. Giving this some thought I can agree... sweat, tears and most especially the sea. Tears don't come easy for me, probably because as a child I was told to "dry it up before I give you something to cry about'; so hot yoga provides an opportunity to sweat. And if I ever move, it will be closer to the sea.

As I walked the shore line I was looking for perfect, unbroken seashells, with pretty edges. I noticed more broken ones, with rough and rugged edges, than perfect ones. Then, there were the broken ones which had been smoothed by the continuous caressing of the ocean waters flowing in and out, over and over again. It was then I realized how I am like the broken shells. Life experiences have broken me and left me rough. Yet here I am. As I recognize the brokenness and jagged edges, I can also see a smoothing of my broken edges. How unconditional love from Jerry gives me a place to re-center when the pain of my childhood rears its ugly and unnerving head. How yoga guides me to be centered and mindful, to focus on my breath and to trust myself. It fills the void of the missing self-esteem and strengthens my self-confidence. Smartsafe has equipped me mentally, emotionally and physically to protect myself. Although there are moments of struggle, I know I Am Xena!

I am good enough. I am beautiful. I am confident and strong. I am worth advocating for. I am worth protecting. I Am Priceless.

Meditation helps me acknowledge and quiet the inner demons which seek to destroy my efforts to live my legacy. God directs my path toward healing. I stand for myself. I stand for all. As I give voice to the unspoken atrocities of my past, I give voice to so many others who have yet to find their own voices. Voices of Victory. As I pull the skeletons of shame, confusion and self-blame from the silent closets, I help others do the same. Individually and together we are crumbling these generational skeletons. We are making magnificent, life inspiring stepping stones and #HealingForward, sharing strength, peace and joy.

As I sit on the beach finding peace and comfort, with my toes swirling, digging and playing in the alluring, white sands, I'm listening to the melody of waves crash in and watching the sunrise paint peaceful hues of blue and yellow- bright and golden- over the Atlantic. It is time to begin this letter to you, Carla.

{Carla, whether you ever recognized it or not, you were one of my abusers. I'm not sure how old I was when you chose to be my dad's mistress; maybe I was 5 years old. As a woman myself and having been married for over 30 years, it baffles me how you were content being The Mistress. I'm certain your own lack of strength and confidence directly influenced you to verbally and psychologically abuse me. I was a reminder that you were not his wife, and it is when we are weak that we try to tear others down.

Carla, I was just a child; young, weak, impressionable, needing unconditional love, protection, wise guidance. I needed mature adults who accepted responsibility for their actions instead of blaming me or others for the wrong in their lives.

You were emotionally damaged. I don't know your childhood. I don't know much about you at all. Yet, as an adult now, I know there had to be experiences in your own life where you felt controlled, belittled and not good enough. How else could you resign yourself to being The Other Woman? To make yourself feel better you used emotional blackmail and head games on me, tearing me down, leaving me insecure and fearful.

Earlier this year, you and your daughters, Sue and Aime reached out to me virtually. I had not thought of you all for many years. If it had just been Sue I may have interacted with her. But you, you unsettled me and brought old emotions up from the dark crevices of my unpleasant past. A past I don't want to revisit! Yet, here I am four months later still exploring, expressing and learning how to #HealForward. I was happy, strong and confident in my abilities and life calling. In a blink of an eye, I was reduced to an insecure, doubting and miserable child again. All I wanted to do was stop living! The agony- so strong. I didn't want to think. I didn't want to interact with others. I did not want to feel. I did not want to live.

Do you realize in your later years, what a damaging effect you've had? I'd ask if you care, but the tone of your email let me know that you still think destructively. Karma is a bitch. How miserable you must be. Thank you for helping me uncover this darkness so I may find healing and better live my purpose.}

August 11, 2015

Having just read the article *Calm Horizons* in *Yoga Journal July 2015* magazine, I am able to recognize how I have lived in a long term state of anxiety; a persistent, unrealistic and at times excessive worry about measuring up, being good enough, being able to do it all, and to not make mistakes. Being criticized, made fun of, or ridiculed for being human and making mistakes is crippling. It truly is a wonder I haven't been medicated. At the same time, it's no wonder I hit the unrelenting wall of adrenal fatigue and have dealt with chronic muscle tension.

August 14, 2015

It's been 41 years since Cheri died. Decades of life without my older sister and first friend. I will never know how much she protected me from or how much she suffered. Was she violated like I was? Being a brittle diabetic, living in an emotionally abusive home, it's understandable she was in and out of the hospital. Understandable she may have intentionally allowed herself to slip into a coma; just to get away from it. While I may never know the truth of her existence or passing, I do know I have missed her immensely. Concrete Angel, stay close.

I have taken this afternoon to get away from the office and home. Looking for the opportunity to express emotions, I have slipped away to the pool to swim and write. Finding my ability to overcome the shadows of my past. It is time to write this letter to one of my perpetrators.

{Adam, you along with my dad used me. Your inappropriate and selfish sexual desires preyed upon my child innocence. You took advantage of my gentle spirit and desire to obey authority.

You need to know how I have suffered. And as I write this I wonder how many other survivors you have left in the shadows of your assaults. How many found the strength and courage to speak out against you? Did any of them get justice for your wicked and vile use of their young bodies and naïve minds? Questions I may never have answers to. Just the same, the strength of my warrior princesses, bursts forth. Deep in my soul, a rumble begins to rise and I know Xena is finding strength to move forward again, to equip and empower me.

Adam, did you ever recognize the pain you inflicted upon me? Did you ever have remorse? Did you force yourself on Cheri? So much went to a grave of silence with her. I know in many ways she was my protector. You were such a prick and a total jackass. A liar. A pedophile. A rapist. You stole my childhood. You made me uncomfortable and afraid. As a child of 11 or 12, I didn't have the words to express my anxiety. Anxiety that has haunted me for four decades.

I lacked the confidence or strength to advocate for myself. I didn't even know I needed to. The 5 years between your assault and the authorities being notified *are an empty slate in my mind*. I simply existed. As an adult, and as family, YOU should have been my protector, not my perpetrator. There is no excuse for your behavior. If I could, even all these years later I would allow you to rot in prison or die by lethal injection. I would allow fellow prisoners to violate your lousy ass and fulfill your worst wicked imagination. How, I hope you burn in an everlasting hell, if there is one. One way or another, may you ever suffer, be in unrequited pain, anguish and may you never find peace for your mind or emotions.

The scriptures say the sins of the father are upon their children. I'm not in a place to trust The Bible as infallible. Yet, I know your son was following in your steps. He made a move on another family member when she was around 8. Generational abuse.

Oh, the turmoil I have dealt with because of you! As I write this letter, I know you will never read it. I'm simply venting what has never been voiced before. This letter is a stepping stone on my #HealingForward journey. I realize hatred is real. I hate you. I acknowledge this without apology, knowing it is part of the process of cleaning an old, festering wound.}

Letter to my dad. I didn't think to date this entry.

{Dad, do I call you that? I guess by default.

The years of grooming, conditioning me to live within the figurative box; the box of a hostage, left me in a trance of scarcity. Instead of embracing possibilities with spunk and excitement, I would see challenges to be endured or done away with. Instead of discovering, embracing and expressing my brilliance and creativity, I displayed the by-products of oppression, isolation, exclusion and constant defeat. Of course, these by-products fit your manipulative and controlling mindset.

Dad, I acknowledge you were a confused by-product of your own childhood, your personal choices and societies teachings. At the same time, you were the adult. You had a sense of right and wrong, you had the chance to make different choices. Your emotional, psychological and sexual abuse of me caused lasting damage. Children are impressionable. As a child, my heart was to be obedient, make you happy and proud. I would do whatever was expected without question. I trusted you and accepted your skewed ideas of love and obedience.

I have struggled without, and cried for, the beautiful, healthy father-daughter relationship you failed to provide. Over and over again I felt like I was at a dead end, which led to frustration, confusion, anxiety and hopelessness. Anxiety, oh the years of unrecognized anxiety! And the fear, debilitating fear of making a mistake. Do you know, I am just coming to recognize this fear and anxiety. Just being able to tell myself, 'mistakes are good, they are part of the process. Relax. It is ok. You are not broken.' Of course you don't.

Far too long I have unwittingly closed myself from building bridges of hope. I have lived most of my life in a state of overwhelm, attracting and embracing despair. Dad, your mixed messages: 'Work hard. Study. Make good grades, etc. along with your mind games tearing me down, were crippling. I accepted the fallacy of lack, struggle, and separation as unavoidable, just the way of life.

Encouragement, compassion and unconditional, fatherly love would have set me on a different path. A path of peace for the journey, along with the confidence and courage to live authentically.

At this point in time, I understand more of who I have always been. As I recognize this, I struggle to fully say YES to myself. Yet, I know I'm living a lie if I don't. I cannot change what happened. I cannot bring back the past. However, I can change the future by being strong and confident. I can inspire and equip others to #HealForward, overcoming the past and creating a more peaceful future.

Best-Selling Author, Marianne Williamson, has many quotes and poems which help me express my inner struggles. Through her book *Return to Love*, she helps me recognize my power. The culture of my childhood and society in general was to reduce self-esteem. Dad you reinforced this fallacy. This long standing myth negated my worth and confidence, instead of helping me embrace my brilliance, beauty, and talents. Afraid to be powerful and frightened by my light, I have lived in darkness. My son and daughter-in-law often respond, "I'm fabulous." when I ask how they are. Independently of each other, they inspire me with their brilliance and confidence. Through them, I am better able to grasp and live my own fabulousness. What I now recognize, is everytime I let my own light shine, I unconsciously give others permission to do the same. As I #HealForward, I am liberated from my fear and my presence automatically liberates others.

As I continue to seek truth, I continue to uncover ways to heal and move forward. Because of you, I am dedicated to equipping society against domestic violence and sexual assault.

Dad, you took my voice way from me consistently as a child. I was a piece of property to be used. One repeated experience, which had a serious impact on me was your insistence to see my breasts to 'make sure they are developing properly.'. Even now, writing this, the shame and frustration from my adolescent years stirs within me. My feeble attempts to protest or express my discomfort were quickly brushed away with your distorted justification, 'I'm your father, I have been seeing you your whole life.'

For so many years I have harbored resentment and anger toward you. Now, I understand the painful effects this has had on my health. I am so tired of striving. The internal discord has led to poor health and wasted energy. *I want, yea need, to be in control of my mind and emotions.*

When I first thought about writing this letter to you, I expected it to be a verbal thrashing, full of venom and fire. Yet, at this point, on my healing journey I feel compelled to release; just exhale and release. It's time for me to inhale life. Inhale space. Inhale peace. So I can exhale peace. I must be the change I want to see in the world.

I want, yea need, liberty, freedom of mind and peace within that I may more effectively help others find their own way forward. So I may finally be free of physical pain and limiting beliefs. So as a society we can begin shifting the tide and live above and beyond the effects of domestic violence and sexual assault.}

{From www.YogaHope.org: 'You gain strength, courage and confidence by every experience in which you really stop to look fear in the face. You must do the thing you think you cannot do.' ~Eleanor Roosevelt

Feelings of fear and guilt in the body build up, leading to shame. Shame sometimes forms during childhood when we can't change things happening to and around us. We continue to blame ourselves and feel fundamentally flawed and unworthy of love. As adults we have difficulty accepting kindness. Feelings of shame are a way we protect ourselves from being rejected. 'What we can see depends mainly on what we look for.'}

Brene' Brown writes on the connection between shame and perfectionism in *The Gifts of Imperfection*. It was eye opening information and I have found my truest gifts: courage, confidence and connection when I embrace my imperfections.

Finding My Voice October 2015

I'm grateful to have met with a dear friend today. Her reminders really helped me re-center and embrace the fact "people don't understand me or where I am coming from; and "it's ok!". I'm a wavemaker." What a difference it makes when even one person believes in me. Encouragement is oxygen to the soul. Thank you Dear Friend. I appreciate you!

It was a difficult day when someone I trusted, in an environment where I had, up till this experience, felt was safe from life's abusive ways, made assumptions about me, questioned my integrity and verbally attacked me. Accusations, including 'victim blaming' and teaching from a place of fear instead of empowerment were expressed. Wow, the flood of emotions - the disbelief, left me reeling. This was coming from the one person I thought would always seek understanding and refrain from judgment. The accusation of 'victim blaming' felt like a knife was jabbed into my heart and twisted. What a blow to my character and self-esteem. I found myself questioning my thoughts, my strengths and my knowledge. This incident led to a large knot behind my knee which took a couple of days to begin diminishing. Just one more realization my emotional health directly impacts my physical health.

This individual and I spoke and cleared the assumptions and misunderstandings. Now, I am moving forward with greater desire to find a way to address emotional and mental anguish *before* they are manifested in my physical body. Easier said than done, yet I must continue to try. I remind myself, 'My voice is necessary. I express myself with clear intent. I hear and speak the truth. Creativity flows in and through me.'

I am on a search for the answer to why I crumble into a victim mindset and begin self-destructing when I receive an emotional attack. I spoke with my counselor regarding this incident. She asked me to consider if there was even a thin thread of truth to the 'fear' statement. I was able to honestly say how fear does surface when I'm learning something new, until I'm confident in my knowledge/skill. Yet in regard to my ability to defend myself and when I am empowering other women, I am confident. When I mentioned the accusation of 'victim blaming' my counselor was taken aback and momentarily speechless. Then she said, "Believe what a person does, not what they say." "Consider their energy. Is it an energy you want to be around?". Valuable insight and important reminder, *actions override words*. Always believe what someone does over what they say, when their words and actions don't match.

I know we are all human and make mistakes, mis-read people, make assumptions and can be emotional. I have trusted this person. I have believed I was in a safe, non-judgment place. I believed it was okay to be authentic, let my guard down regarding my recent struggles. Yet, this emotional set back has been painful and difficult to overcome.

For my own wellbeing, it is time for me to embrace forgiveness. To truly let go. So today I journal providing an outlet for my emotions and thoughts. I am on a journey to embrace life with compassion, through strength and confidence. Compassion for myself and honoring myself. Compassion and respect for those who hurt me. My intention, finding peace with myself; extending peace to others. To be the change I wish to see in the world. By making the journey ourselves, we can guide others.

November 4, 2015

#HealingForward is intentional. Being aware of this and desiring to be purposeful with my thoughts, I began using this mantra: Inhale: Embrace the present. Exhale: Release the past. Finding joy and protecting peace on this journey from Survivor to Thriver.

Dr. Wayne W. Dyer, from *I Can See Clearly Now*. talks about being able to understand how the encounters, challenges and situations in life, are all exquisite threads in a tapestry representing and defining life. He also expresses his gratitude for all of it. While I have learned to be grateful for most of life's encounters, I'm still learning in other areas of life.

December 15, 2015

Growth and awareness occurring daily as I #HealForward, reminding myself to be the change I wish for the world. I am reminded as we studied intentions and vibrations at yoga teacher training, the critical relationship between Thoughts → Words → Behavior → Habits → Values → Destiny. It is important to keep them positive!

While I have not been one to embrace 'spirit animal' teachings, I was recently impressed to at least look into the symbolism of the dragonfly. Time after time, in a large assortment of settings, dragonflies crossed my path. Their beauty and purpose left me marveling. My take away; embrace opportunities for change, explore my emotions with a joyful and light approach, look through illusions and ask, are the person's intentions clear or deceiving? Just as dragonflies change colors as they mature, I need to be open and willing to change as I mature.

How interesting this message of change continues to unfold? The book, *The Gifts of Imperfection*, is guiding me to a whole hearted life and that allows me to embrace who I am. My random wisdom card, 'I am willing to change.'. It is my goal to release the habit of assuming and communicate, ask questions. My mantra: I express myself with clear intent.

December 25, 2015

The sun is finally breaking through the morning fog here at Corpus Christi. Truly I am grateful to be sitting on the beach. The sea birds are crowded around keeping me company. One vocal friend cries for handouts. I wasn't thinking when I tossed a couple of bad grapes. Now she wants more and she brought her flock of beach friends.

I find joy in the gulf mist dampening my hair. Feeling the breeze caressing my skin is refreshing as the sun's warmth takes the chill out of the air. The sand covering my feet like fine sugar glistening on cookies. Walking the beach, feeling the energy of the environment, finding peace during the frustrations of life and relationships. This, is where I need to be.

Thoughts of what it would be like to have enjoyed a healthy childhood fluttered through my mind and hoovered in my heart this morning. To have experienced unconditional, healthy love... What is love? Love should mean peace, happiness, joy; especially joy. According to Merriam-Webster, Love is a noun. A feeling of strong or constant affection for a person. From *Psychology Today*, love is used in many levels: to love a partner romantically; to love a sibling as a confidant; my pet opens my heart to love; and time on the beach makes me feel relaxed and happy.

A New Year... January 3, 2016

'I am here at the right time.' in a season of regeneration. The work I do on myself is not a goal, it is a process... a lifetime process. I choose to find joy through the process.

Change is inevitable, growth is optional. If there is one thing I have found through reading *The Gifts of Imperfection*, I am not alone. There is an entire society embracing 'boxed-in' thinking, trying to find inner peace while living by someone else's definition and expectations for their life. I'm letting my own light shine, so others may do the same, and together, we can make a difference. Meaningful change is a process, uncomfortable, messy and risky. Yet, I'm grateful for the information and opportunity to cultivate authenticity and calm. Excuses Be Gone!

It is through the windows of perception that we see others and form life opinions from these views. Life experiences impact the condition of our windows. Are they clean, dirty, smudged, and cracked? Are they clear or foggy? **May we choose soft cloths of gentleness, peace and love, when cleaning the smudges and fog; be gentle with ourselves and with others.**

Excuses Be Gone! January 17, 2016

'Be in the now!' This, is the moment I have. Time is simply a series of present moments. If I fill my head with frustrating or angry thoughts about what is happening or the way the world looks to me, I'm not going to have a very good relationship with life.

Blaming others for deficiencies or any conditions of my life keep me from fulfilling my own highest destiny. Lessons from Dr. Wayne W. Dyer in *Excuses Begone*, we all do exactly what we know how to do given the conditions of our lives; and what we surrender to becomes our power.

I have the power to move forward by questioning my thoughts. I can ask, 'Is it true?' 'How does this thought serve me?' and then let go of the mind viruses, so I can heal. Or, I can hold onto old thoughts, viruses and the associated suffering. My body, like everything else in life, is a mirror of my inner thoughts and beliefs. Every cell responds to every single thought I think and every word I speak. Either way, my mind is a powerful force; one for good and healing or for pain and suffering.

So often survivors emphatically state, 'I am not a victim!' While each of us has been victimized, our choices and mindset direct whether we think like victims, survivors or thrivers. Regardless of what we state, our actions can still betray a victim mindset. While what happens to us can change us, we can refuse to be reduced by it.

Often, what we need to process, we hold as tension in our bodies. As I become more aware of this I utilize yoga, meditation, and journaling to work through and move beyond the thoughts and emotions which no longer serve me.

It is self-defeating to embrace negative thoughts toward others. I am only hurting myself. Studying and researching have brought me to the realization, *this negative energy hurts me physically*. Learning to let go of expectations in a relationship is painfully difficult. So I ask myself, 'Do I really want to hold onto a habitual thought → behavior which ultimately makes me sick?' When I'm able to process my response it is a resounding, 'No'. I really do want to use my free will and precious currency of life, *time*, to be the change I wish to see in the world.

The Shift, movie March 16, 2016

The real purpose of life is to be happy. Happiness is when my thoughts, words and actions are in harmony.

I found the following information from *The Shift* interesting and personally applicable. A quantum moment leading to a shift in life has four qualities: it is vivid, surprising, benevolent and enduring. It turns life upside down. The movie reveals a woman's top priorities prior to and after a quantum moment. I totally related. Before the moment: family, career, fitting in, our values are wrapped up in our attractiveness; after: personal growth, spirituality, sense of self-esteem, happiness and forgiveness.

The quantum moment for me occurred on a regular, clear Spring morning in April of 2009. I share the details of this account in *Share Your Message With the World, Vol. 1*. It is still a vivid impression in my mind. I was caught by surprise how easily and fervently I relayed my desire to empower women as their first line of defense. Over the valleys of despair and through the challenges of finding my path, the driving force endures exhaustion and discouragement. I am happiest when I am living in harmony with this quantum moment, my shift.

April 14, 2016

It is during life's greatest challenges that we can find deeper powers within ourselves.

Like fire, self-doubt, can consume everything in its path and affect every area of our lives. Self-doubt can produce a state of not thinking clearly and the inability to focus our attention. This can cause potentially disastrous pain and suffering for ourselves and others. Understanding this concept is such a freeing moment. 'I am confident and strong.' 'Trust yourself.' are messages I still use today to overcome this debilitating mind set when it surfaces.

Real inner transformation can occur when I deliberately investigate why I act or react the way I do. Understanding long standing behavioral patterns and what caused them provides the opening I need to change the way I think and act. Change is a natural part of nature. Stagnation goes against the ebb and flow of nature.

In our body, stagnation is evident as muscles tighten up, opinions become rigid and habits solidify. In yoga, doing asanas with enough effort to release heat is a priceless discomfort which is good for us. Considering new ideas and behaviors, creates heat as our brain circuits are rewired. By consciously challenging long-standing behaviors we allow the opportunity for growth. These are positive changes and we should welcome them.

On this journey, as I learn when and how to use my voice, life seems to be providing more challenging experiences. My voice is important, even when others don't understand. Another difficult and painful life event has provided the opportunity to speak up, be a voice and although I did; after the fact, behind closed doors, I was sobbing a pool of tears, with snot flowing, and my body shaking. It may take me the rest of my lifetime to work through a childhood of abuse and decades as an adult mistakenly thinking I was okay.

An old familiar saying, If you don't like something, change it. If you can't change it, change the way you think about it. Journaling has become part of learning to change the way I think about things I can't change. So step by step, I can #HealForward and "Be the change I wish to see in the world..."

A dear friend shared the following while teaching a class I had the privilege of attending. 'After you peel away your thoughts, consciousness remains and this is who you are.' It impressed me and led to the following thoughts. Use a soft cloth; words of love and encouragement, self-compassion, to clear the smoggy film left from years of pollution. Violence like pollution has an adverse effect. We need to be gentle with ourselves as we peel away our thoughts and see our true reflection.

'It takes time and effort to uncover a treasure.' YOU are worth far more than this world's treasures. You Are Priceless. Be kind, patient and long suffering as you discover and embrace your personal worth.

Brene' Brown, Ph.D., L.M.S.W. so giftedly describes what I have lived with in her book, *The Gifts of Imperfection.* She describes the difficulty in owning my story, and how much more difficult it is to spend my life running away from it. Yet, by exploring the darkness, I am able to discover the infinite power of my light. Such an enlightening and encouraging read.

Own your story. Love yourself. Walk away from shame. Embracing the process is one of the bravest things you will ever do. Extend grace to yourself and embrace your vulnerability with tenderness. Claim your power.

#HealingForward has been messy, painful, soul shaking and precarious. There have been numerous times when I felt my whole life and relationships were hanging in the balance. Consistently, I felt like the only means of survival was to walk away from everyone and everything. Why do I tell you this? Because it is real and another survivor feels the very same way. Sometimes, walking away is the choice made as a means of survival. A decision difficult for some to understand.

These feelings have been opportunities for me to dig into the root, uncover and cut out the problem. You can too. This journey of discovery and recovery require tenacity, grit, courage, deep levels of self-compassion, and regular, unrelenting self-advocacy. The process can be uncomfortable for those around you as well. Recognize and discuss this process with them so they can better support you. Walking away from those who love you *is not* the only means of survival.

Cultivating my authentic self, means speaking up for issues I once spoke against. Seeing injustice for what it is. Recognizing the greatest risks lie in remaining silent. By speaking up I give voice to situations where inherent human rights are either ignored or even worse, violated and treated unfairly, simply because of a general, long-held belief system.

To some, I have changed. I'm a different person than I used to be. These individuals never knew me beyond the surface. Inside, I'm the same strong spirit. From my current perspective, I see this vocal woman, who for the first time in her life is willing to persistently embrace her truth and passionately share this truth, to live on purpose. To unapologetically be true to herself, for herself and to inspire others to do the same. To no longer be content with mediocrity and excuses. To no longer be silenced because my thoughts are not valued or my words make someone uncomfortable.

One day, I may be a grandmother and I am determined to do all I can to create a better me. So I may equip and empower my grandchildren. I simply MUST be the change I wish to see in the world. Together, we are stronger. Together, we are creating change. Otherwise, as through years and decades past; I would hurt myself and create confusion for others. I would continue to perpetuate injustice to myself, by myself and from others; as well as by myself toward others.

Fear, scarcity and uncertainty were my captors. Feelings of inadequacy and suffering are a shared human experience. By facing my fears, getting facts, educating myself and taking action-speaking up... I am creating a new reality for myself and others.

It has been my long held, deep desire to enlighten, equip and empower female survivors of abuse. This desire and my journey of #HealingForward have led to the birth of the I Am Priceless movement. For just as a single foot step does not create a path; a single thought, a single action will not create a new path. It is when multiple steps are taken, a new path is created. As we provide new thoughts and continuous action, we create new paths for ourselves and others. If this resonates with you, join us at www.IAm-Priceless.org and together we can create healthy, mental paths leading to societal change.

Ralph Waldo Emerson has a quote about people only seeing what they are prepared to see. So I ask, are you ready to see yourself as good enough? As Beautiful? Confident? Courageous? Are you ready to see yourself as more than able? Worth advocating for? Worth protecting?

Let me remind you; You ARE Beautiful. You ARE Confident. You ARE Courageous. You ARE more than able! You ARE worth advocating for. You ARE worth protecting. You ARE Priceless!

It's time to start asking yourself, "How is my story serving me? Does it bring me peace or inner turmoil? Does it help me love myself and others or lead to unkind, hateful thoughts and actions? When an old story, an old belief, which no longer serves us is set on repeat, the endless tape loop continues to negatively impact our actions and behaviors. Our personal breakthroughs begin with a change in beliefs.

We always have options. We get to choose how we will deal with situations and how we will feel about it. Having an open mind about attitudes, helps us make situations, ones that are painful and/or unpleasant, into a learning or growing experience. When situations which have previously left us struggling emotionally arise, we can now look around and ask, 'How can I make this into a wonderful experience? What can I think – feel – say – do to learn from this?' We get to outgrow the victim mindset. Dr. Wayne Dyer reminds us we are the ones, only ones, who must decide to take suggestions and turn them into behvior which is constructive and self-fulfilling.

YOU can choose to #HealForward. You Are Priceless!

About Regina Rowley

Regina Rowley is an engaging speaker, international bestselling author and instructor of women's self-defense at KUTA! Empowered Women. As a women's self-defense specialist with a Black Belt in Taekwondo, *and her favorite certification:* Smartsafe Instructor, Level 4, Regina is continuously advancing her knowledge and skills.

Regina is an international voice bringing awareness to violence against women and exposing generational skeletons hidden in closets. She is effecting change by enlightening and empowering survivors with support to *#HealForward* in *I Am Priceless, Voices of Victory Over Violence.* As a bestselling author in *Share Your Message with the World* and in *Behind Her Brand* Regina inspires and encourages others to live life on purpose. www.IAm-Priceless.org was founded by Regina to equip, support and empower women on their #HealingForward journey. Please join us.

Regina will inspire and empower your audience to overcome limiting beliefs. "Confidence is the unconquerable enemy of fear." ~Regina Rowley

Book Regina Today
http://www.iam-priceless.org/request-a-speaker/

- www.IAm-Priceless.org
- www.ReginaRowley.com
- regina@reginarowley.com
- @ReginaRowley / #ViolenceStopsHere
- 805-VOI-CE89

You are beautiful and you are loved.

Domestic Violence Survivor

For Women Everywhere, by Terri St. Cloud, used with permission.

Please visit and support: www.bonesigharts.com where Terri provides such poignant truths, in stirring words and simple art.

This poem echoed through my person so strongly when I read it, I reached out to meet Terri; seeking permission to share with you, our beautiful readers. Perhaps it will resonate with you too.

<u>For Women Everywhere</u>

something snapped inside of her.
'ENOUGH ALREADY!' she screamed.
it's time for women everywhere to
claim their worth, their value,
their beauty, their sacredness.
no more of this believing the
darkness that's been thrust upon
them.
no more taking the blame for the
sins of others.
no more claiming themselves failures
when in fact, they are survivors.
it's time for women to stop.
turn around.
face those people who have hurt,
harmed, and wounded and let them
know that they refuse to be destroyed.
they refuse to carry the burden.
it's time for women everywhere to

claim their power, their beauty
and their right to shine.
it's time for women everywhere to
place the palms of their hands on
their wounds, acknowledge the pain
and change the world with the lessons
gained from that pain.
it's time to move with the wisdom
of a survivor and to know your strength.
the world is waiting for us.
let us step up now and reclaim ourselves,
and reclaim the world.

Made in the USA
San Bernardino,
CA